5-Minute Feasts

Stir-Fry Gourmet Cooking for Two

5-Minute Feasts

Stir-Fry Gourmet Cooking for Two

by Karl Wurzer

Contemporary Books, Inc.
Chicago

Design by Joseph Trautwein

Illustrations by Judith Fast

Copyright © 1980 by New Century Publishers, Inc.
All rights reserved
Published by Contemporary Books, Inc.
180 North Michigan Avenue, Chicago, Illinois 60601
Manufactured in the United States of America
Library of Congress Catalog Card Number: 81-71077
International Standard Book Number: 0-8092-5738-6

Published simultaneously in Canada by
Beaverbooks, Ltd.
150 Lesmill Road
Don Mills, Ontario M3B 2T5
Canada

This edition published by arrangement with
New Century Publishers, Inc.

Contents

To the Point

THIS BOOK IS DEDICATED to the belief that what this country needs is a good five-minute dinner. For the working couple or for people who live alone—for all those who are pressed for time, dining can and should be just as elegant as for those who have all day to dabble in the kitchen.

The recipes in this book have all the grace and charm of the finest epicurean cuisine without the time-consuming hours of preparation. All of these dishes serve two people, cook in five minutes or less, and require minimal preparation. Each recipe can easily be doubled or tripled to serve more.

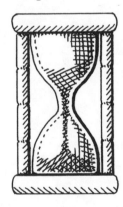 These recipes are primarily Westernized versions of Oriental stir-fry dishes with an added variety of flavor combinations ordinarily found only in the finest European and Indian dishes. Prepare one of these original dishes to break the monotony of serving packaged dinners sold in supermarkets or take-out dinners that wind up cold or soggy. The following five-minute meals are superior in flavor as well as convenience, primarily because they are cooked quickly. This method preserves their freshness and taste as well as a wealth of nutrition that's constantly being demolished by overcooking in the typical American kitchen.

Variety is an added advantage to this selection of recipes, which ranges from appetizers to desserts. There are exciting soups and quick egg dishes, including a new approach to preparing omelets that are as foolproof as they are simple and elegant. A luscious selection of crêpes is offered. There are rice and pasta dishes, salads, and main courses of fish, shrimp, lobster, beef, pork, chicken, liver, lamb, and veal. And all can be cooked in five minutes or less! The entrées are superb with or without accompaniments. Any of the quick vegetable dishes or sauces can turn a simple broiled steak or chop dinner into a real feast.

These recipes can be lifesavers when you're in an unexpected rush; you'll enjoy not only the speed and simplicity they offer but their stimulating variety. Each dish is truly impressive and memorable— a five-minute feast.

BEFORE
YOU BEGIN

Basic Needs

Very little basic equipment is needed to create your five-minute feasts. Most of the dishes are cooked in either a 10-inch or a 12-inch frying pan. A blender is required to prepare ingredients for some recipes.

Herbs and Spices

One of the most effective weapons to combat monotony in quickly cooked dishes is a well-armed herb and spice rack. Remember that spicy food and well-spiced food are not synonymous.

These dishes are enhanced by well-balanced and individualistic spicing that is inspired by many great cuisines of the world to give you a truly broad spectrum of flavor.

The herbs and spices used in the following recipes have been carefully chosen to give your meals the flair they deserve. There's no more effective, or inexpensive, way to achieve startling variety in cooking than by judicious seasoning.

Stocks

Stocks are second only to herbs and spices as the most important single tool in creating fine cuisine, especially in quick cooking. Traditionally, the preparing, finishing, and cooking of stocks have been very time-consuming. This is unnecessary—particularly when the stocks are added simply to extend the already flavored pan sauce of meat and fish dishes. This book includes recipes for quick beef, chicken, and fish stocks. They have excellent flavor and require a minimum of ingredients. The stocks are also salt-free, only mildly spiced, and almost completely fat-free—all of which adds to their versatility.

An excellent way to store stock is to first boil it down to half volume, which can be accomplished to some degree during normal cooking. Then freeze this double-strength stock in ice-cube trays and transfer the stock cubes to plastic bags. The stock is then available for instant use in any quantity and occupies just half the freezer space it would at normal strength. There is another advantage to double-strength stock cubes. If you need, for example, one cup of stock for a recipe, simply put enough double-strength cubes in a measuring cup to occupy about ½ cup, then add tap water to complete the amount. This allows exact measurement without having to defrost the stock, and the tap water quickly defrosts the stock cubes.

If you prefer not to make your own stocks, use canned broths or bouillon for chicken and beef. For fish stock, substitute half clam juice (canned) and half dry white wine. Unfortunately, most commercially packaged broths and bouillons are much too salty. Low-salt products may be found in a supermarket, health-food store, or specialty store that offers foods for people restricted to particular diets. Whether or not you're salt-conscious in your diet, the commercial broths detract from the freshness and subtlety of flavor in any recipe.

Still another alternative to making your own stocks is to add homemade or commercially canned chicken or beef gravy to any dish that calls for chicken or beef stock that is thickened at the end with a starch slurry. Again, the flavor will not equal that of fine stocks, but it will be acceptable.

Food Preparation and Cooking Tips

Here are some basic procedures for preparing and cooking ingredients quickly and efficiently.

Eggs, beaten   When beaten eggs are called for in a recipe, usually to coat food prior to frying it, they can best be made by breaking the eggs into a bowl and beating them with a fork or whisk. This takes only a few seconds and once beaten the eggs stay usable for hours. Do not use an electric mixer or blender to beat eggs that will be used to coat foods; the result is inferior and leaves you an unnecessary cleanup job as well.

Cheese, grated   By far the best grated cheeses are those you grate yourself just before using. Commercially packaged cheeses may be inferior products initially and are not enhanced at all by their sitting on a shelf for months. They are, of course, convenient. However, it's also fairly convenient to buy freshly grated cheese at the deli departments of supermarkets or at specialty stores and cheese shops.

Chives   Chives and green onion tops can be chopped, dried, and then frozen in plastic containers. One containerful should keep you supplied for a long time and needs no defrosting before use. (The chopped chives are easily removed from the container, provided they're dry when frozen.)

Garlic   To save time, you may substitute crushed garlic cloves for minced garlic cloves. Just remember to discard them at the end of cooking, unless you like whole pieces of garlic in your cooking. Whole garlic tends to lose most of its strength even in quick recipes. If you use garlic powder, which lacks the fresh and rounded flavor of the cloves, use about one-quarter the amount specified in the recipe for fresh garlic.

Onions   Onions can be chopped or minced and then frozen in quantity in plastic containers. To chop a fresh onion by hand, first peel it, then cut off the top half-inch or so. Make parallel cuts through two-thirds of the onion, then give it a quarter turn and crosscut into the onion, creating a cross-hatched effect. Next turn the onion on its side and slice through the crosshatching. Cut only the amount you need at the moment. Wrap the rest of the onion in waxed paper and refrigerate it. If you use dried onion flakes, use about one-quarter the amount specified in the recipe for fresh onion.

Celery and peppers Celery and green and red peppers can be chopped or minced in quantity and then frozen.

Herbs ground in a mortar It takes only a few seconds to grind leafy herbs in a mortar, which definitely enhances their flavors in the cooked dish. Rubbing the herbs between your palms directly over the pan is even quicker and almost as effective. Seeds, such as caraway or poppy, can be ground in a mortar or cracked quickly by pressing them with the flat side of a heavy knife on a hard surface.

Tomatoes For added speed and convenience, use tomato purée in place of fresh tomatoes. For the equivalent of 1 cup of fresh chopped tomatoes, use a scant ½ cup of tomato purée. (You will lose some of the fresh flavor, of course.)

Toasting nuts or coconut The quickest and simplest way to toast nuts or coconut is to stir them constantly in a dry pan over medium heat. Once they start to color, remove them from the heat since they burn rather easily. Another method, which ensures more even browning, is to spread the nuts or coconut on a dry baking pan and to toast them in a medium oven (350°F), tossing occasionally. I recommend toasting coconut in a large frying pan and toasting fresh, unsalted nuts in the oven. (Commercial dry-roasted nuts are a convenient alternative.)

Meats To cook quickly, meats must be in thin pieces. Cutting across the grain will yield the most tender results. Some butchers will prepare meat in this way or you can do it yourself. Trimming away excess fat and slicing a pound of stewing beef chunks, or any other large piece of meat, into thin slices takes only minutes with practice. In an hour's time, you can trim and cut all the meats you'll need for a couple of weeks. Partially freezing meats helps in cutting thin slices. Then just freeze them in daily portions.

Liver Liver slices of about ¼ inch thick are ideal and should be turned just once during cooking. Cook each side just a minute or so to retain the moisture inside. Liver is almost always overcooked, even in so-called fine restaurants. Not only the texture but the flavor suffers, which becomes harsher the longer the meat cooks. Of course, chicken and pork livers must be fully cooked but try not to overdo it—or simply don't use them. A good choice is calves' liver, which should be just slightly pink inside when done.

Chicken The chicken recommended in these recipes is boneless and skinless breast meat, cut into ⅛-inch-thick slices. You can use any other lean chicken meat, of course, or the lean meat of any other fowl, such as turkey. Leftover meat can be used in any recipe. If it's a bit difficult to cut the chicken to the recommended thickness of ⅛ inch, cut ¼-inch-thick slices. They cook almost as fast.

Fish   For best results, fish fillets should be about ¼ inch thick. However, even at ½ inch thick, they will cook quickly in any seafood recipe. The main problem with fish is its tendency to break up. Do not stir the fillets vigorously as you would meat; gently turn them once during cooking. Thin fillets of any fish need to be cooked only a minute or so on each side to be completely done and to absorb all the flavors of the pan sauce.

Shellfish   Precleaned lobster, shrimp, or crabmeat chunks may be used interchangeably in any seafood recipe. For shrimp or lobster, however, the flavor is enhanced by using pieces with the shells left on. The simplest way to clean shrimp or lobster tails is to split them lengthwise with a sharp heavy knife and then wash out the dark central veins (intestines). Or, cut through the tops of the shells with scissors, starting at the fleshy end; cut into the flesh just deep enough to expose the vein and then wash it under running water, leaving the shells on and otherwise intact. Lobster tails can also be cut crosswise at the joints of the shells.

Clams and oysters   Canned clams or oysters can be used in place of fresh; the canning juices may be substituted for fresh clam or oyster liquor.

Measurements   All measurements within these recipes can be considered approximate. You needn't spend a great deal of time making sure you use *exactly* one cup of chopped onion or one teaspoon of parsley. Measuring cups and spoons are certainly recommended but only to provide approximate amounts. With a little experience you'll soon be measuring ingredients by hand, which will save a tremendous amount of preparation time. Get used to estimating measurements—it's the relaxing way to cook!

Butter   Butter is not recommended for general use in these recipes. It is considered the least healthy of all cooking fats commonly used today because it is animal fat, which is highly saturated and contains cholesterol. Vegetable-based margarines and oils are preferred, since they are much lower in saturated fat and contain no cholesterol whatever. Nor do vegetable fats scorch as easily as butter, which makes them better for quick cooking over high heat. Be careful when buying margarine. Much of it has been hardened, or hydrogenated, which is a process that improves the margarine's texture and shelf life but changes its unsaturated fat to saturated fat. Look for vegetable margarines that are not hardened or hydrogenated (or at least only partially so). Using vegetable oil in place of margarine in any recipe also eliminates saturated fat.

Adding stock to partially cooked ingredients   Generally, the recipes in this book recommend that any stocks added during the cooking of a dish be hot so as not to lower the temperature of the partly cooked dish and slow the cooking time. Simply heat the stock while you tend to the rest of the cooking. Or, if you haven't room for the extra pot on your stove and must add cold stock to a partly cooked dish, add it in a slow stream, stirring all the while. This will allow the stock to heat almost instantly on contact with the large surface of the pan and will not affect your cooking time more than a few seconds.

Slurries   A slurry is a mixture of starch and liquid, such as cornstarch dissolved in a little cold water. To thicken any pan sauce with a slurry, add a little of the hot pan sauce to the slurry *before* adding the slurry to the pan. This allows the starch to begin to absorb the liquid and raises the liquid's temperature closer to that of the pan sauce, thus preventing lumps and speeding the thickening process. You may need to add more or less slurry than is indicated in the recipe. For example, frozen foods that exude water during cooking require more thickening; dishes that are cooked very hot may dry out and require less.

Seasoning   At various times throughout the cooking process, test each recipe for proper seasoning and make any necessary adjustments.

Cooking times   All cooking times in this book, as in any other, should be considered approximate. The general rule to follow is to cook an ingredient just until it is done—additional cooking will lessen its nutritional value and the freshness of its flavor. This is also true for pork and chicken, which should be thoroughly cooked but not overdone.

Stir-Fry History and Technique

Stir-fry cooking dates back thousands of years to the very beginnings of Chinese society. Long before any similar "culture" was born in the West, the structure of China's diverse classes coalesced to produce huge masses of peasants supporting the elite.

Within this society, it became customary for farmers to move away from their villages in spring to live in temporary huts near the fields in which they would work until fall. This yearly isolation, and somewhat nomadic existence, necessitated some adjustments in the farmers' cooking, both to save time and to limit the amount of utensils. The problem was further complicated by a scarcity of fuel, since the finest farming areas were soon treeless expanses, field after field, from horizon to horizon. The few bushes that sprouted between fields or from the dikes separating rice paddies were generally wet with sap in the spring, and what little dead wood was available in the form of dried twigs was exhausted within a few days. The dung of the draft animals could be used for fuel, but only after a rather long drying process in the sun. Its supply was also much too meager. Obviously, the bulk of the fuel needed for cooking had to be brought from a distance, and the more extensive the farming of an area became, the farther the peasants had to go for that fuel. This was the birth of stir frying—cooking that can be completed in just minutes, using a single pan over a fairly small fire. Farmers began stir frying meats or vegetables to which they added cooked rice that was brought from the villages once or twice a week. This combination produced a very efficient field menu.

Stir-fry cooking can best be described by a simple basic recipe, one that could be used to cook virtually anything:

OIL

FLAVORINGS

MEATS AND/OR VEGETABLES IN THIN SLICES

1. *Heat the oil in a pan or wok over fairly high heat.*

2. *Add spices and seasonings to taste.*

3. *Add meats and/or vegetables and fry, stirring briskly, until done (2 to 5 minutes).*

Stir frying is an ideal cooking technique for any foods except those that are notoriously uncooperative in regard to speed, such as carrots and turnips.

Actually, the addition of spices to the oil in a pan before adding meats or vegetables is more an Indian tradition than Chinese. The Indians use a much greater variety in their spicing techniques and this allows the spices to develop their full flavors very quickly. Those flavors can then be transferred rapidly to the meats or vegetables that are added to the pan. This is especially important in stir frying, where time is limited. If the fullness of spice flavor isn't developed quickly, it isn't developed at all.

Physically, cooking any food is accomplished by simple heat transfer. The more quickly the heat is transferred from the source to the food, the more quickly the food will cook. Thus it is important to stir fry in a large pan so that a good deal of the food to be cooked can be in direct contact with the pan surface at a given time, speeding the heat-transfer process. A secondary effect of heat transfer in stir frying is accomplished by the continual stirring of the foods. When portions of food that have been heated by contact with the pan are stirred to mix with still uncooked portions, heat is transferred from the hot pieces to the cold and initiates their cooking. Therefore, steadily stirring the food in a pan over high heat will cook it evenly and in the shortest time.

A wok may be used in any of the stir-fry recipes in this book in place of a pan. Personally, I prefer a pan for several reasons. I have found that a pan is more stable on the stove and can be handled more easily. A pan is flat and works better than a wok with a minimum of fat; fat may fall into a pool at the bottom of a wok. Last, a flat pan on an electric stove speeds heat transfer. On the other hand, a wok has the advantage of being an interesting cooking and serving vessel that can be set right on your table.

While stir frying is certainly an extremely simple process, there are a few tips that might save you time or improve your technique:

1. Slice foods as thinly as possible for the fastest cooking.

2. For maximum speed and nutrition, use the highest heat possible without scorching the foods. The more quickly the food is cooked, the less it deteriorates.

3. Try getting used to adjusting the heat as you cook. If an ingredient begins to dry out, lower the heat a bit before it has a chance to scorch. If it isn't cooking fast enough, raise the heat. I often vary the heat several times during a simple five-minute recipe. Before adding stocks, sauces, or any liquid to the pan during the cooking process, first turn the heat higher than you need it. This will help the added liquids heat through quickly. It is especially important to adjust the heat when adding raw meats to a pan, since they tend to "catch," or scorch, easily. Keep the heat somewhat moderate before adding the meats, and once they start to cook you can raise the heat again without the danger of their scorching.

4. Unless you're cooking very frangible foods like fish fillets, stir briskly and try to turn the pieces while you stir to spread the heat evenly.

5. Use enough oil or margarine. If you scrimp on the oil in stir frying, the food will be improperly cooked. In the first place, the oil in the frying pan should be very hot before you add any foods. This will make the food "grab," as in deep-frying, which cooks the outside almost at once and precludes the absorption of excess fat into the food itself. If the oil is hot enough initially, most of it will still be in the pan when you're done. Also, if you don't use enough fat over high heat, parts of the foods you're cooking will not be lubricated properly and will scorch immediately on contact with the pan. (The chemicals in scorched foods are as unhealthy as cigarette smoke.) I'm not suggesting, however, that everything you cook by the stir-fry method be soaked with oil. If you want to reduce the amount of fat in a stir-fried dish, use a pan with a nonstick finish and simply eliminate the margarine or oil recommended in any given recipe, except for a tiny bit to cook any herbs or spices before adding the other ingredients (an excellent trick from Indian cooking). And if you want to eliminate *all* fat, just use a few drops of water or wine or any other liquid to moisten the spices or herbs. Their flavors will develop just as well and add a

remarkable richness of taste, compared to the typical European method of adding spices later in the cooking process. Pans lined with a nonstick finish are excellent for use over high heat.

Fingertip Hints

1. Cook the way *you* want; you needn't follow recipes exactly.

2. Estimate measurements to add speed and relaxation to cooking.

3. Experiment with your own spice and herb combinations.

4. Cook casually; don't worry about exact times or temperatures in stir frying.

5. Simplify any recipe presented here as desired. If you're not too fond of a particular ingredient, substitute for it or reduce its amount or omit it altogether.

6. Substitute ingredients at will. If you're out of apples, pears make an excellent stand-in. Use strawberries in place of raspberries, peaches in place of apricots, and so on.

7. If you don't have a certain wine or cordial that is called for in a recipe, use something similar in taste.

8. If you plan to make a dish ahead of time with a cornstarch-thickened sauce, do not thicken the sauce until just before reheating and serving; otherwise the sauce may lose its thickness.

9. Make allowances for frozen foods that release water as they cook, especially vegetables and fish.

10. Do not let a stir-fried dish become too dry in a conventional pan, or the high heat will scorch the food.

11. The faster a food is cooked (without scorching), the more nutrition is preserved.

12. The thinner the food is sliced, the faster it will cook.

13. Thinly sliced foods absorb flavors more thoroughly.

14. Very high temperatures can dry foods very quickly.

15. Stir frying is most efficient when using a spoon in one hand and a wide spatula or pancake turner in the other, so you can turn the foods completely over while stirring.

16. Nuts and other small solid pieces of food tend to lie on the bottom of a pan and scorch easily.

17. Prepare and freeze chopped onions, celery, and peppers in bulk, as suggested earlier. You'll save hours of preparation time.

18. To reduce or eliminate fats in any pan-cooked recipe, use pans with nonstick finishes.

19. If you substitute dried onion or garlic for fresh, use one-quarter the amount specified in the recipe.

20. Use unsalted or low-salt stocks and broths whenever possible to allow more successful seasoning of dishes.

21. Check the seasoning of each dish after the final cooking.

22. To keep cooked pasta from sticking after draining, mix in about a teaspoon of margarine to coat the strands.

23. Eggs at room temperature will cook much faster and require less cooking fat than those taken directly from the refrigerator. Set out the eggs before starting the recipe; even 15 minutes will warm them considerably and lead to better results.

24. To cook a flat omelet quickly, cover the pan with a lid that fits just inside the pan rim so there is very little space between the eggs and lid. This will speed the cooking time and thus eliminate one of the main problems with flat omelets—their tendency to overcook on the bottom. Cook the omelet in this manner for about 3 to 4 minutes over medium to high heat.

SAUCES AND STOCKS

Creole Sauce *makes ½ cup for meat, fish, vegetables*

3 *tablespoons chopped green pepper*
2 *tablespoons chopped onion*
1 *garlic clove, chopped*
¾ *cup chopped tomato*
salt and pepper to taste
2 *drops hot pepper sauce (tabasco), or ¼ teaspoon chopped chili pepper*
¼ *teaspoon basil*
¼ *teaspoon oregano*
1 *tablespoon margarine*
1 *teaspoon cornstarch blended with 1 tablespoon very thick, rich chicken stock or gravy (or blend cornstarch with 1 teaspoon water)*
1 *tablespoon capers, coarsely chopped*

- Blend green pepper, onion, garlic, tomato, salt, pepper, and hot pepper sauce in a blender for a few seconds.
- Fry basil and oregano in margarine in a small pan over medium to high heat for a few seconds, stirring constantly.
- Add blender paste to spices and fry 3 minutes longer, stirring.
- Add cornstarch and stock slurry and stir briskly for a few seconds to blend and thicken.
- Add capers and mix in quickly. Serve hot.

Gold Sauce *makes ½ cup for meat, fish, vegetables*

½ *cup water*
2 *teaspoons sugar*
2 *tablespoons cider vinegar*
2 *teaspoons prepared horseradish*
1 *tablespoon cornstarch blended with 1 tablespoon Madeira*
2 *egg yolks*

- Heat water, sugar, vinegar, and horseradish in a small pan over high heat, stirring until the sugar is dissolved (about 20 seconds).
- Add cornstarch and Madeira slurry and stir briskly for a few seconds to blend and thicken.
- Remove from heat and let mixture stand for 2 minutes to cool.
- Beat in yolks vigorously. Serve warm.

NOTE: *If you must reheat this sauce, do not let it approach a boil or the yolks will curdle. Reheated, the sauce becomes very thick, like a custard.*

Quick Hollandaise Sauce *makes ½ cup for vegetables*

3 *tablespoons margarine*
1 *egg yolk*
¾ *teaspoon lemon juice*
¾ *teaspoon hot water*
1 *teaspoon warm water, lightly salted*
  pepper to taste

- Melt margarine in a small pan; set aside to cool.
- Blend yolk, lemon juice, and hot water in a blender until foamy.
- Add margarine to yolk mixture in a thin, steady stream with the blender on high speed. Blend well.
- Add warm water to mixture with blender on high speed.
- Add pepper to taste. Blend a few seconds; serve.

NOTE: *This sauce can be made ahead of time and kept fresh for a week or more if made with fresh ingredients and if properly refrigerated.*

Lemon Orange Sauce *makes ¾ cup for fish and meat*

 2 *teaspoons margarine*
⅛ *teaspoon cinnamon*
⅛ *teaspoon coriander*
1/16 *teaspoon nutmeg*
  dash of ground cloves
½ *lemon rind, grated*
½ *orange rind, grated*
  juice of half a lemon
  juice of half an orange
½ *cup Madeira*
½ *teaspoon sugar (or to taste)*
 2 *teaspoons cornstarch blended with 1 tablespoon sour cream*

- Melt margarine in a small pan. Add spices and grated lemon and orange rinds and fry over medium heat for a few seconds, stirring.
- Add lemon juice, orange juice, Madeira, and sugar. Bring to a boil over higher heat.
- Add cornstarch and sour cream slurry and stir briskly for a few seconds to blend and thicken. Serve hot.

Horseradish Sauce *makes ½ cup for meat*

1½ *teaspoons margarine*
1½ *teaspoons flour*
½ *cup milk or cream*
   salt and pepper to taste
1 *tablespoon prepared*
   horseradish (or to taste)

- Melt margarine in a small pan. Add flour and fry over low heat for a few seconds, stirring.
- Add milk and blend in quickly. Cook to thicken over higher heat, stirring constantly for about 1 minute.
- Add salt, pepper, and horseradish; blend in quickly. Serve hot or warm.

Quick Mayonnaise *makes 1 cup*

1 *egg*
1 *teaspoon cider vinegar*
   salt and pepper to taste
1 *teaspoon prepared mustard*
¼ *cup vegetable oil*
¾ *cup vegetable oil*
1 *tablespoon lemon juice*
1 *tablespoon boiling water*

- Blend egg, vinegar, salt, pepper, mustard, and ¼ cup of oil in a blender on medium speed.
- With blender still on medium speed, add ¾ cup of oil in a steady stream.
- Still blending, add lemon juice and boiling water. Serve.

NOTE: *This mayonnaise can be made ahead of time and kept fresh for a week or more if made with fresh ingredients and if properly refrigerated.*

Sesame Sauce *makes ½ cup for meat*

2 *tablespoons sesame seeds,*
   crushed in a mortar
½ *cup chicken stock or broth,*
   heated
1 *tablespoon soy sauce*
½ *teaspoon minced chili pepper*
1 *teaspoon cider vinegar*
2 *teaspoons cornstarch blended*
   with 1 tablespoon cold stock

- Fry sesame seeds for 30 seconds in a pan over medium to high heat, stirring (no fat is needed).
- Remove pan from heat and add stock and soy sauce. Return to heat and fry 30 seconds longer, stirring.
- Add chili pepper and vinegar; blend in quickly.
- Add cornstarch and stock slurry and stir briskly for a few seconds to blend and thicken. Serve hot or at room temperature.

Split-Second Tomato Sauce *makes ½ cup for meat, vegetables*

1 cup coarsely chopped tomato
½ small onion, coarsely chopped
½ garlic clove, chopped
salt and pepper to taste
1 tablespoon margarine
¼ teaspoon parsley
⅛ teaspoon basil
1⁄16 teaspoon oregano
2 teaspoons tomato paste
2 teaspoons cornstarch blended with 2 tablespoons very rich chicken stock or with 1 tablespoon water

- Blend tomato, onion, garlic, salt, and pepper in a blender for a few seconds.
- Melt the margarine in a 10-inch pan. Add herbs and fry over medium to high heat for a few seconds, stirring.
- Add blender paste and tomato paste to spices; fry 2 minutes longer, stirring.
- Add cornstarch and stock slurry and stir briskly for a few seconds to blend and thicken. Serve hot.

Double-Strength Beef Stock *makes 1 quart*

3 pounds chopped or ground lean beef (no fat)
3 tablespoons vegetable oil
2 quarts water
4 carrots, thinly sliced
2 onions, quartered
1 celery stalk, thinly sliced
1 clove
½ teaspoon parsley
⅛ teaspoon thyme
½ bay leaf
2 peppercorns

- Brown the beef in oil in a large pot over high heat, stirring for a few minutes.
- Add remaining ingredients. Bring to a boil slowly and skim fat off top.
- Simmer 2 hours (the liquid should reduce somewhat but still cover the ingredients).
- Pour stock through a strainer, squeezing juices from the meat and vegetables. Return stock to the pot and boil down to 1 quart if necessary. Skim fat off top, dabbing with a paper towel if needed.
- Freeze stock in ice-cube trays and store the frozen cubes in plastic bags.

NOTE: *Ordinarily, beef stock must cook for 6 to 8 hours, then stand in a refrigerator all night so the fat from the beef can rise to the surface and solidify. This must be removed before the stock is stored. But ordinary beef stock uses beef trimmings, bones, and fat, along with the meat. In this quick and easy stock, the use of beef meat alone precludes excess fat in the stock; what little appears is skimmed off at the beginning of cooking. This stock can be clarified by straining through cheesecloth before boiling down.*

Double-Strength Chicken Stock *makes 1 quart*

3 *pounds chopped or ground chicken meat (no fat)*
2 *quarts water*
4 *carrots, thinly sliced*
2 *onions, quartered*
1 *celery stalk, thinly sliced*
1 *clove*
½ *teaspoon parsley*
⅛ *teaspoon thyme*
½ *bay leaf*
2 *peppercorns*

- Put all the ingredients in a large pot. Bring to a boil slowly and skim fat off top.
- Simmer 2 hours (the liquid should reduce somewhat but still cover the ingredients).
- Pour stock through a strainer, squeezing juices from the meat and vegetables.
- Return stock to pot and boil down to 1 quart if necessary.
- Freeze stock in ice-cube trays and store the frozen cubes in plastic bags.

NOTE: *Like beef stock, chicken stock is usually cooked 6 to 8 hours and is made with bones, fat, and trimmings, along with the meat. This excellent quick stock eliminates most of the time and effort needed yet retains its quality. For a perfectly clear stock, strain through cheesecloth before final boiling.*

Double-Strength Fish Stock *makes 1 quart*

4 *pounds lean fish meat, bones, and trimmings (do not use fatty fish)*
2 *quarts water*
3 *carrots, thinly sliced*
2 *onions, quartered*
1 *celery stalk, thinly sliced*
2 *cups dry white wine*
½ *teaspoon parsley*
⅛ *teaspoon thyme*
½ *bay leaf*
2 *peppercorns*

- Put all ingredients in a large pot.
- Simmer 30 minutes, skimming occasionally.
- Pour stock through a strainer, squeezing juices from the fish and vegetables.
- Return stock to pot and boil down to 1 quart if necessary.
- Freeze stock in ice-cube trays and store the frozen cubes in plastic bags.

NOTE: *Fish stock, often called fish fumet, is generally made with dry red wine in place of white when it is used for the color in aspics. For a completely clear stock, strain through cheesecloth before final boiling.*

APPETIZERS
AND SOUPS

Anchovy Dip

1 *tablespoon margarine*
1 *can (2 ounces) anchovy strips,*
   squeezed dry between paper
   towels
2 *garlic cloves, minced*
   pepper to taste
½ *cup sour cream*

• Melt margarine in a small pan. Add anchovies, garlic, and pepper and fry over medium to high heat, mashing with a fork until smooth (about 2 minutes).

• Blend in the sour cream. Serve as a dip for raw carrot sticks, celery sticks, pepper strips, tomato slices, or other crisp vegetables.

Fried Beef (or Pork) Canapés

½ *cup ground beef or pork*
1 *egg*
1 *tablespoon minced or grated*
   onion
   salt and pepper to taste
3 *slices white bread, crusts*
   removed, quartered
3 *tablespoons margarine*

• Mix first 4 ingredients in a small bowl until the meat absorbs the egg.

• Spread mixture on one side only of each bread quarter.

• Melt the margarine in a 12-inch pan. Add canapés, meat side down, and fry over medium to high heat for about 3 minutes. Turn and brown lightly on the other side for about 1 minute. Drain on paper towels and serve hot.

Cheese and Anchovy Bread

4 *slices French or Italian bread,*
   about ½-inch thick, crusts
   removed and with a pocket
   in each
4 *slices cheddar cheese or*
   American cheese
4 *flat anchovy fillets, drained,*
   dried on paper towels, and
   chopped
3 *tablespoons margarine*

• Stuff the bread with cheese and anchovies.

• Melt the margarine in a 12-inch pan. Fry stuffed bread about 2 minutes on each side over medium to high heat, until bread is golden, and cheese is melted. Drain on paper towels and serve hot.

Olive Cheese Bites

16 *plain crackers*
16 *small slices Swiss cheese, cut to same size as the crackers*
 4 *large pimiento-stuffed olives, each cut into 4 slices*

- Preheat oven to 400°F. Spread the crackers on a baking tin and top with the Swiss cheese.
- Garnish cheese with the sliced olives.
- Bake in oven a few minutes, until cheese melts. Serve hot.

Deviled Clams

1 *can (6½ ounces) minced clams, drained*
2 *tablespoons mayonnaise*
3 *slices bread, trimmed and quartered*
3 *slices Swiss cheese, quartered*

- Preheat broiler.
- Mix clams with mayonnaise. Spread mixture on bread and top with cheese.
- Broil on a lightly oiled baking tin until cheese is melted (about 2 minutes). Serve hot.

Clam and Cheese Dip

2 *tablespoons margarine*
2 *tablespoons minced green pepper*
2 *tablespoons minced onion*
1 *can (6½ ounces) minced clams, drained*
2 *slices American cheese, chopped*
2 *tablespoons tomato sauce*

- Melt margarine in small pan. Add green pepper and onion; fry 1 minute over medium to high heat, stirring.
- Add clams, cheese, and tomato sauce; lower heat and fry until cheese melts, stirring (about 2 minutes). Serve hot, in the pan, as a dip for breads, crackers, chips and/or raw vegetable sticks.

Clam Toast

2 *tablespoons margarine*
1 *can (6½ ounces) minced clams, drained*
½ *small tomato, minced*
¼ *green pepper, sliced thinly*
1 *garlic clove, minced*
¼ *teaspoon parsley*
⅛ *teaspoon oregano*
  salt and pepper to taste
4 *slices French or Italian bread, toasted, crusts removed*

- Melt margarine in a 10-inch pan. Add all ingredients except the toast and fry for 3 minutes over medium to high heat, stirring.

- Spread the clam mixture on quarters of the toast and serve hot.

Crab in Cream Sherry

2 *tablespoons margarine*
¼ *teaspoon parsley*
⅛ *teaspoon basil*
⅓ *pound lump crabmeat*
2 *tablespoons cream sherry*
  salt and pepper to taste

- Melt margarine in 10-inch pan. Add parsley and basil and fry for a few seconds over medium to high heat, stirring.

- Add crabmeat and fry 1 minute more, tossing gently. Add sherry, salt, and pepper; fry 2 minutes more, tossing gently. Serve hot.

Crab (or Shrimp) Imperial

1 *tablespoon margarine*
2 *tablespoons minced green pepper*
½ *pound lump crabmeat, or small shrimp, shelled and cleaned*
  salt and pepper to taste
2 *tablespoons mayonnaise*
  a few drops hot red pepper sauce, or Worcestershire sauce to taste (optional)

- Melt margarine in 10-inch pan. Add green pepper and fry for 2 minutes over medium to high heat, stirring.

- Add crabmeat, salt, and pepper; fry 3 minutes more, stirring gently. Let mixture cool.

- Blend crab mixture with mayonnaise and either red pepper or Worcestershire sauce and serve.

Date-Bacon Bites

12 *pitted dates*
12 *cashew nuts, preferably*
   unsalted
 4 *bacon strips, cut crosswise*
   into 3 short strips each

• Stuff dates with cashews.

• Wrap a bacon strip around each stuffed date and fasten with a toothpick lengthwise so the date bites can roll easily.

• Fry until done (about 3 minutes) in a 10-inch pan over medium to high heat, turning constantly. Serve hot.

Quick Liver Pâté

 3 *tablespoons margarine*
½ *teaspoon parsley*
¼ *teaspoon basil*
⅛ *teaspoon oregano*
 2 *tablespoons minced onion*
 1 *garlic clove, minced*
½ *pound chicken livers, chopped*
   and seasoned
 1 *tablespoon brandy*

• Melt margarine in a 10-inch pan. Add herbs, onion, and garlic; fry for a few seconds over medium to high heat, stirring.

• Add livers and fry 5 minutes, stirring and finally mashing livers with a fork while they cook.

• Flame with the brandy, stirring until fire dies. Mold pâté into a small, solidly packed mound and chill. Serve with bread or crackers.

Lebanese Meatballs

½ *pound finely ground lamb or*
   beef
 1 *egg yolk*
 3 *tablespoons finely minced*
   pine nuts
 2 *tablespoons grated or finely*
   minced onion
½ *teaspoon parsley*
¼ *teaspoon mint*
   salt and pepper to taste
 2 *tablespoons margarine*

• Knead all ingredients, except the margarine, together by hand until very smooth.

• Melt margarine in 10-inch pan. Form mixture into tiny meatballs and fry over medium to high heat, turning very carefully, until browned and done (about 5 minutes). Drain on paper towels and serve hot.

Greek Fried Mushroom Caps

2 *tablespoons vegetable oil*
2 *tablespoons chopped onion*
2 *tablespoons chopped celery*
1 *garlic clove, minced*
½ *teaspoon parsley*
¼ *teaspoon thyme*
  salt and pepper to taste
8 to 12 *large mushroom caps*
2 *ounces dry white wine*
1 *tablespoon lemon juice*

- Heat oil in 10-inch pan. Add onion, celery, garlic, parsley, thyme, salt, and pepper; fry for a few seconds over medium to high heat, stirring.
- Add mushroom caps and fry 4 minutes, turning often.
- Add wine and lemon juice; fry 1 minute more, stirring. Serve just the mushroom caps, hot.

Noches

3 *slices American cheese, each cut into 8 triangular pieces*
24 *flat tortilla chips*
24 *small strips of hot green pepper (fresh or canned)*

- Preheat oven to 400°F. Set a slice of cheese on each tortilla chip and top with a pepper strip.
- Bake a couple of minutes, just until cheese melts. Serve at once, hot.

Deviled Nuts

2 *tablespoons peanut oil*
½ *teaspoon garlic powder*
¼ *teaspoon red pepper (cayenne), or to taste*
  salt to taste
½ *cup whole shelled nuts (almonds, pecans, or cashews)*

- Heat oil in 10-inch pan. Add garlic powder, red pepper, and salt; fry a few seconds over medium to high heat, stirring.
- Add nuts and fry about 4 minutes, until browned, stirring constantly. Drain on paper towels and serve hot or at room temperature.

Fried Oysters (or Clams)

12 *oysters or clams*
salt and pepper
flour
1 *egg, beaten*
2 *tablespoons vegetable oil*
2 *tablespoons soy sauce mixed with ½ tablespoon cider vinegar*

- Season oysters with salt and pepper to taste. Dust lightly with flour, then dip in beaten egg.
- Heat oil in 10-inch pan. Add oysters and fry until golden over medium to high heat, turning gently. Serve hot, with soy sauce and vinegar mixture as a dip.

Sweet and Sour Pork Strips

1 *tablespoon peanut oil*
1 *garlic clove, minced*
¼ *teaspoon coriander*
⅛ *teaspoon ginger*
½ *pound small, thin pork slices, salted to taste*
1 *tablespoon cider vinegar blended with 1 teaspoon sugar*
toast, cut into 1-inch-wide strips (optional)

- Heat oil in 10-inch pan. Add garlic, coriander, and ginger; fry a few seconds over medium to high heat, stirring.
- Add pork and fry 3 minutes more, stirring.
- Lower heat. Add vinegar mixture and fry 1 minute more. Serve hot, with toast if desired.

Sardines in Tomato Sauce

1 *tablespoon margarine*
2 *tablespoons minced onion*
1 *garlic clove, minced*
½ *cup tomato sauce*
1 *can sardines, drained on paper towels*
several small lettuce leaves
2 *tablespoons finely minced green pepper*

- Melt margarine in 10-inch pan. Add onion and garlic and fry 1 minute over medium to high heat, stirring.
- Add tomato sauce and fry 30 seconds more, mixing well.
- Add sardines and turn very gently to heat through. Serve hot, on lettuce leaves, sprinkled with green pepper.

Nippy Scallop Fry

2 *tablespoons Italian olive oil*
½ *small chili pepper, minced, or*
   to taste
2 *tablespoons minced onion*
1 *tablespoon minced fresh*
   parsley, or ½ teaspoon
   dried parsley
1 *tomato, chopped*
   salt to taste
½ *pound scallops, sliced*
¼ *cup pitted black olives, halved*
1 *teaspoon chopped capers*

- Heat oil in 12-inch pan. Add chili pepper, onion, and parsley; fry a few seconds over medium to high heat, stirring.

- Add tomato and salt and fry 30 seconds more, stirring. Then add scallops and fry 3 minutes more, stirring.

- Mix in olives and capers and fry a few seconds to heat through. Serve hot.

Shrimp Cakes

½ *pound shrimp, shelled,*
   cleaned, chopped, and
   mashed with a fork
4 *ounces canned water*
   chestnuts, drained,
   chopped, and mashed with
   a fork until pastelike
½ *very small scallion, minced*
1 *teaspoon candied ginger,*
   minced
1 *egg yolk*
½ *teaspoon cornstarch*
   salt and pepper to taste
3 *tablespoons margarine*

- Blend all ingredients except margarine, until smooth, mashing together with a fork.

- Shape mixture into small, thin cakes.

- Melt margarine in 12-inch pan. Fry shrimp cakes over medium to high heat until done (about 3 minutes). Serve hot.

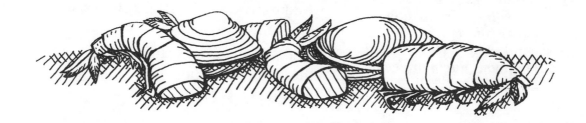

Anise Shrimp

2 *tablespoons peanut oil*
½ *teaspoon anise seeds, crushed*
   in a mortar
½ *pound medium to small*
   shrimp, shelled and cleaned
   salt and pepper
2 *tablespoons soy sauce blended*
   with 1 teaspoon hot red-
   pepper sauce

- Heat oil in 10-inch pan. Fry anise seeds for a few seconds over medium to high heat, stirring.
- Add shrimp and fry 2 minutes more, stirring.
- Season with salt and pepper to taste. Fry 1 minute more, stirring. Serve hot, with soy-sauce mixture as a dip.

Shrimp Toast Squares

¼ *pound shrimp, shelled,*
   cleaned, chopped, and
   mashed with a fork
2 *water chestnuts, chopped and*
   mashed until pastelike
1 *egg white*
2 *teaspoons soy sauce*
½ *teaspoon sherry*
3 *slices white bread, crusts*
   removed, quartered
3 *tablespoons margarine*
   duck sauce (optional)

- Mash together first 5 ingredients with a fork.
- Spread mixture on the bread, coating one side only.
- Melt margarine in 12-inch pan. Fry the bread, coated side down, until lightly browned (about 2 minutes), over medium to high heat. Turn bread over and fry about 1 minute more. Drain on paper towels and serve hot, with the duck sauce if desired.

Shrimp in White Wine

1 *tablespoon Italian olive oil*
1 *garlic clove, minced*
½ *teaspoon parsley*
   salt and pepper to taste
½ *cup dry white wine*
12 *large shrimp, cut halfway*
   through and deveined,
   shells left on

- Heat oil in 10-inch pan. Add garlic, parsley, salt, and pepper; fry a few seconds over medium to high heat, stirring.
- Add wine and shrimp; fry 3 minutes more, until shrimp are just done, stirring and turning to cook evenly. Serve hot.

Fried Tuna Canapés

2 *tablespoons margarine*
French bread (about 2 inches in diameter), cut into 10 thin slices, crusts removed
½ *can tuna fish, drained*
2 *teaspoons lemon juice*
1 *tablespoon chopped fresh parsley*
2 *tablespoons mayonnaise*

• Melt margarine in 12-inch pan. Fry bread over medium to high heat until lightly browned on one side only. Drain on paper towels.

• Blend tuna, lemon juice, parsley, and mayonnaise. Spread on untoasted side of bread. Serve hot or at room temperature.

Welsh Rabbit

1 *tablespoon margarine*
1 *garlic clove, minced*
½ *pound cheddar cheese, chopped*
½ *cup beer or ale blended with 1 egg yolk*
1 *teaspoon Worcestershire sauce, or to taste*
¼ *teaspoon prepared mustard salt to taste dash red pepper (cayenne) French or Italian bread, cut into large pieces or strips for dipping, toasted*

• Melt margarine in 12-inch pan. Fry garlic for a few seconds over medium to low heat, stirring.

• Lower heat slightly. Add cheese and mash with a fork while it melts.

• Add beer and yolk mixture gradually, blending in well and beating with a fork.

• Blend in Worcestershire, mustard, salt, and red pepper; cook over somewhat higher heat to thicken, stirring constantly. Do not allow to boil or the yolk will curdle. Serve hot, in a bowl or from the pan, as a dip for the warm toast.

Avgolemono

1 *cup chicken stock or broth, preferably unsalted*
¼ *cup quick-cooking rice salt and pepper to taste*
¾ *cup chicken stock or broth, preferably unsalted*
2 *egg yolks, beaten*
2 *teaspoons lemon juice*

- Boil chicken stock. Add rice, salt, and pepper. Cover and set aside for 5 minutes.
- Bring the ¾ cup chicken stock almost to boiling in a pan over medium to high heat.
- Beat a small portion of this hot stock into the yolks with a fork. Then, beat the yolk mixture into hot stock and cook to thicken lightly, stirring briskly. Do not boil or the yolks will curdle.
- Add lemon juice and mix well.
- Add rice to soup mixture in pan; mix well and serve hot.

Green Bean Soup

2 *tablespoons margarine*
1 *tablespoon chopped fresh parsley, or 1 teaspoon dried parsley*
2 *tablespoons minced onion*
1 *garlic clove, minced*
1 *package (9 ounces) frozen green beans, thawed salt and pepper to taste*
½ *teaspoon paprika*
1½ *cups chicken stock or broth, preferably unsalted, boiling*
½ *teaspoon cider vinegar*
1 *tablespoon cornstarch blended with 1 tablespoon water*
2 *tablespoons sour cream*

- Melt margarine in 12-inch pan. Fry parsley, onion, and garlic for 30 seconds over medium to high heat, stirring.
- Add beans, salt, and pepper; fry 3 minutes more, stirring.
- Mix in paprika well. Add chicken stock and vinegar; cook 1 minute more.
- Blend in cornstarch and water slurry to thicken, then remove from heat. Blend in sour cream and serve hot.

Cream of Asparagus Soup

1 *tablespoon margarine*
1 *package (10 ounces) frozen*
    asparagus, thawed
1 *cup milk or ½ cup each*
    milk and cream, hot
  salt and pepper to taste

- Melt margarine in 10-inch pan. Fry asparagus for 2 to 3 minutes over medium to high heat, stirring.

- Purée asparagus, milk, salt, and pepper in a blender. Reheat in pan if necessary and serve hot. If desired, strain soup before serving.

CREAM OF PEA, BROCCOLI, OR SPINACH SOUP

Proceed as for Cream of Asparagus Soup, substituting a thawed 10-ounce package of frozen peas, broccoli, or spinach for the asparagus.

CREAM OF TOMATO SOUP

Proceed as for Cream of Asparagus Soup, substituting 2 chopped tomatoes and their juices for the asparagus. Cook the tomatoes 4 to 5 minutes, mashing with a fork while stirring. Strain the soup before serving.

CREAM OF CELERY SOUP

Proceed as for Cream of Asparagus Soup, substituting 3 cups very thinly sliced celery stalks for the asparagus and adding another tablespoon of margarine for the frying. Prepare this soup in a 12-inch pan.

Almond Cream Soup

¾ cup chopped blanched
      almonds
1 tablespoon chopped onion
¼ teaspoon coriander
1 cup milk or cream
¾ cup chicken stock or broth,
      preferably unsalted
   salt and pepper to taste
2 egg yolks, beaten
   pinch of grated lemon rind

- Purée almonds, onion, coriander, and milk in a blender until very smooth (blend for several minutes).

- Strain purée into a 10-inch pan. Add stock, salt, and pepper. Heat almost to a boil over medium to high heat, stirring.

- Beat a small portion of the soup into the yolks, using a fork or whisk. Then beat yolk mixture into soup to thicken lightly, stirring briskly. Do not boil or yolks will curdle.

- Mix in grated lemon rind. Let stand for a few seconds off heat, stirring. Serve hot.

Beef Broth with Asparagus

1 tablespoon margarine
1 small scallion, chopped
¼ teaspoon ground ginger
½ package frozen asparagus
      spears, thawed and cut
      into 1-inch lengths
¼ cup sliced mushrooms
1½ cups beef stock or broth,
      preferably unsalted,
      boiling
1 tablespoon sherry
1 tablespoon soy sauce
   pepper to taste

- Melt margarine in 10-inch pan. Fry scallion and ginger for a few seconds over medium to high heat, stirring.

- Add asparagus and mushrooms; fry 3 minutes more, stirring gently.

- Add beef stock and sherry; cook 30 seconds more.

- Season with soy sauce and pepper. Serve hot.

Bouillabaisse

3 tablespoons margarine
¼ teaspoon rosemary
⅛ teaspoon thyme
⅛ teaspoon savory
½ pound shrimp, shelled and
    cleaned
¼ pound thin cod fillets
¼ pound thin flounder fillets
¼ pound thin red snapper fillets,
    or eel fillets
  salt and pepper to taste
¼ cup chopped onion
1 garlic clove, minced
½ teaspoon grated orange rind
1 tomato, chopped and mashed
    with a fork, juices reserved
½ cup canned sliced mushrooms,
    drained
2 cups fish stock (or ⅔ cup each:
    clam juice, dry white wine,
    water), boiling
  French or Italian bread,
    lightly toasted

• Melt 2 tablespoons of the margarine in 12-inch pan. Fry herbs for a few seconds over medium to high heat, stirring.

• Add shrimp, cod, flounder, snapper, and salt and pepper; fry 4 minutes more, over slightly lower heat, turning gently. Set aside.

• Melt remaining tablespoon of margarine in 10-inch pan. Fry onion, garlic, and orange rind for 30 seconds over medium to high heat, stirring.

• Add tomato and its juices, mushrooms, and salt and pepper to 10-inch pan; fry 3 minutes, stirring occasionally.

• Combine tomato mixture and fish stock with seafood in 12-inch pan; cook 1 minute more, without breaking fish fillets. Serve hot with lightly toasted bread.

Bacon and Bean Purée

1 tablespoon margarine
½ teaspoon parsley or chervil
¼ cup chopped, lean Canadian
    bacon, or ham
¼ cup minced onion
2 tablespoons minced celery
1 can (15 ounces) butter beans,
    or kidney beans, drained
  salt and pepper to taste
¾ cup milk, hot

• Melt margarine in 10-inch pan. Fry parsley, bacon, onion, and celery for 30 seconds over medium to high heat, stirring.

• Add beans, salt, and pepper; fry 3 minutes more, stirring.

• Purée in a blender with the milk. Serve hot.

Cauliflower Soup

1 *tablespoon margarine*
1½ *teaspoons chopped fresh parsley, or ½ teaspoon dried*
1 *package (10 ounces) frozen cauliflower, thawed and cut into bite-size pieces*
1¼ *cups chicken stock or broth, preferably unsalted, boiling*
   salt and pepper to taste
1 *tablespoon cornstarch blended with 1 tablespoon water*
2 *tablespoons sour cream*

- Melt margarine in 10-inch pan. Fry parsley for a few seconds over medium to high heat, stirring.
- Add cauliflower and fry 2 minutes more, stirring. Add boiling chicken stock and salt and pepper; cook 2 minutes more.
- Blend in cornstarch and water slurry to thicken. Remove from heat.
- Blend in sour cream and serve hot.

Chicken Corn Soup

1 *tablespoon margarine*
1 *chicken supreme (one side of a whole breast, boned and skinned), diced*
½ *package frozen corn, thawed*
1¾ *cups chicken stock or broth, preferably unsalted, boiling*
   salt and pepper to taste
4 *teaspoons cornstarch blended with 2 tablespoons sherry*
1 *egg, beaten*

- Melt margarine in 10-inch pan. Fry chicken and corn for 3 minutes over medium to high heat, stirring.
- Add boiling stock and cook 1 minute. Season with salt and pepper.
- Add cornstarch and sherry slurry to thicken, stirring soup well. Dribble in the beaten egg, stirring. Serve hot.

Chicken Liver Soup

1 *tablespoon margarine*
¼ *pound chicken livers, cut into bite-size pieces*
½ *cup thinly sliced bamboo shoots*
¼ *cup lettuce strips*
1½ *cups chicken stock or broth, preferably unsalted, boiling*
1 *tablespoon sherry*
2 *teaspoons soy sauce*
  pepper to taste

- Melt margarine in 10-inch pan. Fry livers for 3 minutes over medium to high heat, stirring.
- Add bamboo shoots and lettuce; fry 2 minutes more, stirring. Blend in boiling stock and sherry.
- Season with soy sauce and pepper. Serve hot.

Chicken and Raisin Soup

2 *tablespoons margarine*
1 *tablespoon minced onion*
1 *tablespoon minced celery*
¼ *teaspoon parsley*
⅛ *teaspoon basil*
1 *cup chopped lean chicken meat, well-seasoned*
1½ *cups chicken stock or broth, preferably unsalted, boiling*
¼ *cup raisins*
¼ *cup sweet white wine*
½ *teaspoon sugar*
1 *teaspoon lemon juice*
1 *tablespoon cornstarch blended with 1 tablespoon water and 1 tablespoon sour cream*

- Melt margarine in 10–inch pan. Fry onion, celery, and herbs for 30 seconds over medium to high heat, stirring.
- Add chicken and fry 3 minutes more, stirring.
- Add raisins, wine, sugar, and lemon juice to the boiling chicken stock; cook 4 minutes, stirring as much as possible.
- When chicken is done, add stock to the pan. Then blend in the cornstarch, water, and sour cream slurry to thicken. Serve hot.

Chili Soup

3 tablespoons margarine,
    divided
1 can (1 pound) red kidney
    beans, drained
  salt and pepper to taste
1½ cups chicken stock or broth,
    preferably unsalted
½ cup tomato purée
¼ teaspoon parsley
¼ teaspoon basil
⅛ teaspoon oregano
1 teaspoon chili powder
¼ teaspoon cumin
½ cup chopped onion
¼ cup minced green pepper
¼ cup minced celery
2 garlic cloves, minced
½ pound lean ground beef
  dash red pepper (cayenne)
1 teaspoon Worcestershire
    sauce, or to taste

- Melt half the margarine in 12-inch pan. Fry drained beans, and salt and pepper to taste in half of the margarine for 5 minutes over medium to low heat, stirring occasionally. (Add a little water toward end of cooking if needed; beans should be fairly dry but not scorched.)

- Meanwhile, heat chicken stock; add tomato purée and mix well.

- Melt remaining half of margarine in 10-inch pan. Fry herbs, spices, onion, green pepper, celery, and garlic for 30 seconds over medium to high heat, stirring.

- Add beef and a dash of red pepper to the 10-inch pan; fry 3 minutes more, stirring.

- Add beef mixture, stock mixture, and Worcestershire sauce to the 12-inch pan; mix well with beans and serve hot.

Clam Bisque

1 tablespoon margarine
1 can (6½ ounces) minced
    clams, drained, juices
    reserved
1½ cups milk, or 1 cup milk plus
    ½ cup cream, hot
½ cup dry white wine
  salt and pepper to taste
2 egg yolks, lightly beaten

- Melt margarine in 10-inch pan. Fry clams for 2 minutes over medium to high heat, stirring.

- Add reserved clam juice, milk, wine, salt, and pepper; bring quickly to a boil. Then remove from heat.

- Blend a small portion of soup into the yolks, beating with a fork or whisk. Then blend the yolk mixture into the soup and return to heat to thicken lightly, beating steadily. (Do not let soup approach a boil or yolks will curdle.) Serve hot.

Fish Soup

1 *tablespoon margarine*
1 *tablespoon minced celery*
1 *tablespoon chopped onion*
1 *garlic clove, minced*
½ *teaspoon parsley*
¼ *teaspoon basil*
⅛ *teaspoon thyme*
½ *bay leaf*
1 *cup tomatoes, chopped and mashed, juices reserved*
1 to 2 *teaspoons cider vinegar (optional)*
salt and pepper to taste
1½ *cups fish stock (or ¾ cup each of clam juice and dry white wine), boiling*
½ *pound small, thin fish fillets (sole, cod, snapper, trout, any kind or a mixture)*

- Melt margarine in 10-inch pan. Fry celery, onion, garlic, and herbs for 30 seconds over medium to high heat, stirring.
- Add tomatoes and fry 1 minute more, stirring. Season with vinegar, salt, and pepper.
- Add fish stock and fish; cook 3 minutes more. Discard bay leaf and serve hot.

Flounder Vegetable Soup

1 *tablespoon margarine*
1 *tablespoon chopped scallion*
1 *teaspoon minced candied ginger*
¼ *cup sliced mushrooms*
¼ *cup lettuce strips*
¼ *cup slivered bamboo shoots*
½ *pound flounder fillets, cut into small pieces*
1½ *cups chicken stock or broth, preferably unsalted, boiling*
salt and pepper to taste
2 *teaspoons cornstarch blended with 1 tablespoon sherry*
soy sauce

- Melt margarine in 10-inch pan. Fry scallion and ginger for a few seconds over medium to high heat, stirring.
- Add mushrooms, lettuce, and bamboo shoots; fry 1 minute more, stirring.
- Add flounder and fry 2 minutes more, tossing gently. Add boiling chicken stock and cook 1 minute more.
- Season with salt and pepper. Blend in cornstarch and sherry slurry to thicken. Serve hot and season with soy sauce to taste at the table.

Garlic Soup

1 *tablespoon margarine*
5 *garlic cloves, minced*
¼ *teaspoon parsley*
2 *tablespoons dry white wine*
2 *cups beef stock or broth,*
  preferably unsalted, boiling
salt and pepper to taste
2 *eggs*
1 *slice French or Italian bread,*
  toasted lightly, trimmed
  and cubed
grated Parmesan cheese to
  taste

- Melt margarine in 10-inch pan. Fry garlic and parsley for 30 seconds over medium to low heat, stirring.

- Add wine, boiling beef stock, salt, and pepper; return to gentle boil over higher heat.

- Add eggs and poach. Then, add bread and cook a few seconds more. Serve hot, sprinkled with Parmesan cheese.

Meatball Soup

¼ *pound lean ground beef*
2 *tablespoons bread crumbs*
½ *egg*
½ *tablespoon grated Parmesan*
  cheese
½ *teaspoon minced fresh parsley*
  or chives
½ *teaspoon minced celery leaves*
salt and pepper to taste
2 *cups seasoned beef stock or*
  broth, boiling gently in a
  pot

- Mix first 7 ingredients well, kneading by hand until egg is absorbed.

- Form mixture into tiny meatballs (¾-inch diameter) and drop them into boiling stock.

- Boil 5 minutes. Serve soup hot.

Oriental Mushroom Soup

1 *tablespoon margarine*
¼ *cup diced lean ham*
¼ *cup slivered bamboo shoots*
1 *cup sliced mushrooms*
¼ *cup peas*
1½ *cups chicken stock or broth,*
   preferably unsalted,
   boiling
1 *tablespoon cornstarch*
   blended with ¼ cup dry
   white wine
   salt and pepper to taste

- Melt margarine in 10-inch pan. Fry ham and bamboo shoots for 30 seconds over medium to high heat, stirring.

- Add mushrooms and peas; fry 3 minutes more, stirring.

- Add chicken stock and boil 1 minute.

- Blend in cornstarch and wine slurry to thicken. Season with salt and pepper and serve hot.

Onion Cream Soup

1 *tablespoon margarine*
1½ *cups thinly sliced yellow*
   onions
1 *cup chicken stock or broth,*
   preferably unsalted,
   boiling
½ *cup cream*
   salt and pepper to taste

- Melt margarine in 10-inch pan. Fry onions for 4 minutes over medium to high heat, stirring.

- Add chicken stock, cream, salt, and pepper; cook 1 minute more. Serve hot.

Peanut Butter Soup

1 teaspoon margarine
2 tablespoons minced celery
1 tablespoon minced onion
1½ cups chicken stock or broth,
    preferably unsalted,
    boiling
6 tablespoons smooth-style
    peanut butter blended
    with ¼ cup cream
  salt to taste

- Melt margarine in 10-inch pan. Fry celery and onion for 30 seconds over medium to high heat, stirring.

- Add boiling chicken stock. Then blend in the peanut butter and cream mixture (first blend some soup with the peanut butter mixture, then add the mixture to the pan). Heat through, cooking a few minutes.

- Season with salt. Strain if desired and serve hot.

Sour Pork Soup

½ cup slivered lean pork
¼ cup sliced mushrooms
¼ cup slivered bamboo shoots
1½ cups chicken stock or broth,
    preferably unsalted,
    boiling
1 bean curd cake, about 4
    ounces, sliced (optional)
1 tablespoon cider vinegar, or
    to taste
2 teaspoons soy sauce, or to
    taste
¼ teaspoon hot red-pepper
    sauce, or to taste
2 teaspoons cornstarch
    blended with 1 tablespoon
    water
1 egg, beaten

- Add pork, mushrooms, and bamboo shoots to boiling chicken stock and boil 2 minutes.

- Add bean curd, vinegar, soy sauce, and red pepper sauce; boil 1 minute more.

- Blend in cornstarch and water slurry to thicken. Dribble in egg, stirring. Serve hot.

Pork, Egg, and Watercress Soup

1½ *tablespoons margarine*
¼ *pound lean pork, slivered*
½ *cup coarsely chopped*
    watercress
1½ *cups chicken stock or broth,*
    preferably unsalted,
    boiling
    salt and pepper to taste
2 *eggs*

- Melt margarine in 10-inch pan. Fry pork for 2 minutes over medium to high heat, stirring.
- Add watercress and fry 1 minute more, stirring.
- Add boiling stock and salt and pepper.
- Add eggs and poach until done. Serve hot.

Potato Soup

2 *tablespoons margarine*
2 *tablespoons minced onion*
1 *garlic clove, minced*
1½ *cups finely chopped potatoes*
    salt and pepper to taste
1 *cup chicken stock or broth,*
    preferably unsalted,
    boiling
    chives

- Melt margarine in 10-inch pan. Fry onion, garlic, potatoes, salt, and pepper for 5 minutes over medium to high heat, stirring and covering as much as possible to speed the cooking.
- Purée potatoes and stock in a blender. Serve hot, garnished with chives.

NOTE: *This soup is also excellent served chilled, as a variation of vichyssoise. Since the chilled soup will be thicker, blend in cold milk to reach the desired thickness.*

Snow Pea Soup

¼ *cup diced shrimp*
¼ *cup slivered lean pork*
1 *package (6½ ounces) frozen*
    snow peas, thawed
1½ *cups chicken stock or broth,*
    preferably unsalted,
    boiling
1 *tablespoon soy sauce*
    pepper to taste

- Add shrimp, pork, and snow peas to the boiling chicken stock; boil 5 minutes.
- Season with soy sauce and pepper. Serve hot.

Scallop Chowder

2 tablespoons margarine
½ teaspoon parsley
¼ teaspoon basil
1 cup finely minced potatoes
½ cup chopped onion
    salt and pepper to taste
1½ cups milk, or ¾ cup each
    milk and cream,
    simmering
½ pound scallops, seasoned and
    sliced
2 teaspoons chives (optional)

- Melt margarine in 10-inch pan. Fry herbs, potatoes, onion, salt, and pepper for 5 minutes over medium to high heat, stirring. Cover pan as much as possible to speed the cooking.

- Meanwhile, cook scallops in the hot milk.

- When potatoes are done, add milk and scallops. Serve hot, garnished with chives if desired.

Spinach and Bean Curd Soup

1 tablespoon margarine
½ teaspoon minced candied
    ginger
1 tablespoon chopped scallion
½ package frozen spinach,
    thawed
1½ cups chicken stock or broth,
    preferably unsalted,
    boiling
1 bean curd cake, about
    4 ounces, sliced
1 tablespoon sherry
    salt and pepper to taste

- Melt margarine in 10-inch pan. Fry ginger and scallion for a few seconds over medium to high heat, stirring.

- Add spinach and fry 3 minutes more, stirring.

- Add boiling chicken stock, bean curd, and sherry; cook 30 seconds more. Season with salt and pepper. Serve hot.

Succotash Soup

1 *tablespoon margarine*
½ *package frozen corn,*
  thawed
½ *package frozen lima beans,*
  thawed
  salt and pepper to taste
¾ *cup chicken stock or broth,*
  preferably unsalted, boiling
¼ *cup cream or milk mixed with*
  ⅛ teaspoon sugar, hot

• Melt margarine in 10-inch pan. Fry corn, lima beans, salt, and pepper for 5 minutes over medium to low heat, stirring.

• Purée half the corn and lima beans in a blender with the chicken stock, cream or milk, and salt and pepper to taste.

• Return purée to the pan and mix with remaining whole corn and lima beans. Serve hot.

Tomato Beef Soup

1 *tablespoon margarine*
¼ *pound thin, lean beef strips*
¼ *cup chopped onion*
⅛ *cup minced celery*
1½ *cups chopped tomatoes,*
  juices reserved
1 *cup beef stock or broth,*
  preferably unsalted,
  boiling
2 *tablespoons tomato sauce*
  (optional)
  salt and pepper to taste

• Melt margarine in 10-inch pan. Fry beef, onion, and celery for 1 minute over medium to high heat, stirring.

• Add tomatoes and their juices; fry 3 mintues more, stirring and mashing the tomatoes with a fork.

• Add boiling beef stock and tomato sauce; cook 1 minute more. Season with salt and pepper and serve hot.

EGGS AND PANCAKES

Herb Fried Eggs

2 tablespoons margarine
2 teaspoons chives
½ teaspoon parsley
¼ teaspoon tarragon
⅛ teaspoon chervil
4 eggs
   salt and pepper to taste
2 toast slices, buttered and hot
1 tablespoon sherry
¼ cup beef stock or broth,
   preferably unsalted
2 teaspoons cornstarch blended
   with 1 tablespoon water

- Melt margarine in 12-inch pan. Fry chives and herbs for a few seconds over medium to high heat, stirring.
- Add eggs, season with salt and pepper, and fry until done. Set eggs on hot toast and keep hot.
- Add sherry and stock to pan and mix, scraping up the juices.
- Blend in cornstarch and water slurry to thicken. Spoon over eggs and serve hot.

Steak and Egg Sandwich

2 tablespoons margarine
¼ pound lean beef, cut into
   small thin strips, seasoned
4 eggs
   salt and pepper to taste
4 toast slices, buttered and hot

- Melt margarine in 12-inch pan. Fry steak for 2 minutes over medium to high heat, stirring.
- Break eggs over steak, season with salt and pepper, and fry until done, covered to speed the cooking. Serve at once, on hot toast, as open-faced sandwiches.

NOTE: *When eggs are almost ready, try topping with thin slices of Swiss cheese; finish cooking until cheese melts and serve at once, hot.*

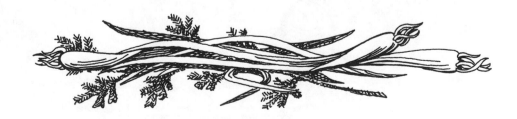

Eggs Benedict

½ cup *Quick Hollandaise Sauce*
   (see **Sauces***)*
1 *tablespoon margarine*
4 *slices lean boiled or baked*
   ham
4 *eggs*
2 *English muffins, split, toasted,*
   and hot
   salt and pepper to taste

- Prepare hollandaise sauce.
- Meanwhile, melt margarine in 10-inch pan. Fry ham over medium to low heat just to warm through.
- Poach eggs in gently boiling water.
- To serve, set hot muffins on two plates; top with ham, then with poached eggs; season with salt and pepper; top with hollandaise sauce and serve at once, hot.

NOTE: *If you wish, garnish with a sprinkling of chopped fresh parsley or chives, or with thinly sliced ripe olives or truffles.*

Eggs Poached in Vinegar and Stock

½ *cup cider vinegar*
1½ *cups chicken stock or broth,*
   or beef stock or broth
4 *eggs*
   salt and pepper to taste
   buttered bread or toast

- Bring vinegar and stock almost to a boil in a pot.
- Add eggs and poach until done. Season with salt and pepper; serve with buttered bread or toast.

NOTE: *For a stronger flavor, use more vinegar and less stock. For milder eggs, use less vinegar and more stock.*

Artichoke Scrambled Eggs

2 *tablespoons margarine*
1 *garlic clove, minced*
½ *cup canned marinated*
    artichoke hearts, sliced
4 *eggs, seasoned, beaten*
    hot toast, spread with
        margarine flavored with a
        little anchovy paste

- Melt margarine in 12-inch pan. Fry garlic and artichokes for 30 seconds over medium to high heat, stirring.

- Add eggs and scramble. Serve hot with toast.

NOTE: *Anchovy paste can be purchased in supermarkets and specialty stores. To make your own, drain a can of anchovies, then mash or grind them in a mortar until perfectly smooth.*

Beef Scrambled Eggs

2 *tablespoons margarine*
1 *cup shredded lettuce*
2 *tablespoons minced onion*
1 *garlic clove, minced*
4 *eggs, seasoned, lightly beaten*
½ *cup slivered lean cooked beef*
    (or use any leftover meat)

- Melt margarine in 12-inch pan. Fry lettuce, onion, and garlic for 1 minute over medium to high heat, stirring.

- Beat meat with eggs briefly; then add both to pan and scramble eggs. Serve at once, hot.

Eggplant Scrambled Eggs

3 *tablespoons margarine*
1 *garlic clove, minced*
¼ *teaspoon dillweed*
    pinch of mace
¾ *cup chopped eggplant*
    salt and pepper to taste
4 *eggs, seasoned and lightly*
    beaten

- Melt margarine in 12-inch pan. Fry garlic, dillweed, and mace for a few seconds over medium to high heat, stirring.

- Add eggplant, salt, and pepper; fry 2 minutes more, stirring.

- Add eggs and scramble. Serve at once, hot.

English Thin Yellow Boys

3 *eggs*
2 *teaspoons finely minced or grated onion*
2 *teaspoons Worcestershire sauce*
1 *teaspoon prepared mustard*
1 *teaspoon cider vinegar*
½ *teaspoon parsley*
¼ *teaspoon tarragon*
   salt and pepper to taste
2 *tablespoons margarine*
4 *slices buttered toast, hot*

- Beat eggs lightly in a bowl with all other ingredients except margarine and toast.
- Melt margarine in 12-inch pan. Scramble egg mixture over medium to high heat.
- Use scrambled eggs as filling for 2 sandwiches on toast and serve hot.

Mushroom Scrambled Eggs

3 *tablespoons margarine*
1 *bacon strip, chopped*
1 *cup chopped or sliced mushrooms, fresh (or ½ cup canned, drained)*
4 *eggs, seasoned, lightly beaten*
   fresh parsley or chives, chopped

- Melt margarine in 12-inch pan. Fry bacon for 2 minutes over medium to high heat, stirring.
- Add mushrooms and fry 1 minute more, stirring.
- Add eggs and scramble. Serve at once, hot, sprinkled with parsley or chives.

Shrimp Scrambled Eggs

2 *tablespoons margarine*
¼ *teaspoon cinnamon*
⅛ *teaspoon nutmeg*
   dash of ground cloves
1 *scallion, chopped*
½ *cup diced shrimp*
4 *eggs, seasoned, lightly beaten*

- Melt margarine in 12-inch pan. Fry spices and scallion for a few seconds over medium to high heat, stirring.
- Add shrimp and fry 1 minute more, stirring.
- Add eggs and scramble. Serve at once, hot.

Tomato Scrambled Eggs

2 *tablespoons margarine*
¼ *teaspoon parsley*
¼ *teaspoon basil*
⅛ *teaspoon oregano*
2 *tablespoons minced onion*
1 *garlic clove, minced*
1 *tomato, chopped, mashed, and drained*
2 *teaspoons soy sauce*
  pepper to taste
4 *eggs, lightly beaten*

• Melt margarine in 12-inch pan. Fry herbs, onion, and garlic for 30 seconds over medium to high heat, stirring.

• Add tomato and fry 2 minutes more, stirring. Add soy sauce and pepper; mix well.

• Add eggs and scramble. Serve at once, hot.

NOTE: *If using a very juicy tomato, you might have to cook it a bit longer to boil away excess moisture before adding soy sauce, pepper, and eggs.*

Avocado Omelet

2 *tablespoons margarine*
½ *of a ripe avocado, pitted, peeled, thinly sliced, and seasoned*
4 *eggs, seasoned, lightly beaten*

• Melt margarine in 12-inch pan. Fry avocado for 1 minute over medium to high heat.

• Add the eggs and cook as a flat omelet. Serve at once, hot.

Cheese and Walnut Omelet

3 *tablespoons margarine, divided*
¼ *cup finely minced walnuts*
4 *eggs, seasoned, lightly beaten*
2 *slices Swiss cheese, chopped*

• Melt 1 tablespoon of the margarine in a small pan. Fry walnuts for 3 minutes over medium to high heat, stirring.

• While walnuts are cooking, melt remaining 2 tablespoons margarine in a 12-inch pan. Start to cook omelet over medium to high heat. Sprinkle with cheese.

• When omelet is nearly done, fill with cooked walnuts, fold, and finish cooking. Serve at once, hot.

Chiffon Omelet

3 *tablespoons margarine*
4 *eggs*
   salt and pepper to taste

- Melt margarine in 12-inch pan over medium heat.
- Break eggs into a blender and season with salt and pepper. Purée eggs for a few seconds, just until they foam a little. Pour eggs at once into the hot pan, cover immediately, and cook about 4 minutes until done, flat or folded. Serve at once, hot.

NOTE: *Add any filling you'd like to this omelet, such as those offered in the recipes for Avocado Omelet, Chili-Dog Omelet, or any others in this book.*

Chili-Dog Omelet

2 *tablespoons margarine*
¼ *teaspoon cumin*
¼ *teaspoon turmeric*
⅛ *teaspoon ground cloves*
¼ *teaspoon chili powder*
¼ *teaspoon celery seeds, crushed in a mortar*
1 *frankfurter, very thinly sliced*
¼ *cup chopped dried figs (optional)*
4 *eggs, seasoned, lightly beaten*

- Melt margarine in 12-inch pan. Fry spices and celery seeds for a few seconds over medium to high heat, stirring.
- Add the frankfurter and figs; fry 1 minute more, stirring.
- Add eggs and prepare a flat omelet. Serve at once while hot.

Hangtown Fry

3 *tablespoons margarine*
   flour
1 *cup shucked oysters, seasoned*
4 *eggs, seasoned, lightly beaten*

- Melt margarine in 12-inch pan. Flour oysters lightly and fry on one side over medium to high heat for about 1 minute.
- Turn oysters over, add the eggs, cover pan, and make a flat omelet. Serve at once, hot.

NOTE: *This omelet is often garnished with crumbled, crisp-fried bacon and/or fried onion rings.*

Pepper and Prosciutto Omelet

2 *tablespoons margarine*
½ *cup minced green pepper*
2 *tablespoons minced onion*
1 *garlic clove, minced*
2 *thin slices prosciutto, chopped*
4 *eggs, seasoned, lightly beaten*

- Melt margarine in 12-inch pan. Fry green pepper, onion, garlic, and prosciutto for 1 minute over medium to high heat, stirring.
- Add eggs and make a flat omelet, covering pan to speed the cooking. Serve at once, hot.

Pork and Pea Omelet

1 *tablespoon vegetable oil*
½ *teaspoon chopped crystallized
    ginger*
½ *cup thin, lean pork strips*
¼ *cup peas*
¼ *cup sliced mushrooms*
1 to 2 *teaspoons soy sauce
    pepper to taste*
2 *tablespoons margarine*
4 *eggs, seasoned, lightly beaten*

- Heat oil in 10-inch pan. Fry ginger and pork for 2 minutes over medium to high heat, stirring.
- Add peas, mushrooms, soy sauce, and pepper; fry 2 minutes more, stirring. Meanwhile, melt margarine in a 12-inch pan.
- Start to cook omelet in the 12-inch pan over medium to high heat. When half-done, fill omelet with cooked pork mixture, fold, and finish cooking. Serve at once, hot.

Salami and Zucchini Omelet

3 *tablespoons margarine*
2 *slices salami, chopped*
1 *small zucchini, thinly sliced*
4 *eggs, seasoned, lightly beaten*
2 *tablespoons grated or shaved
    cheddar cheese*

- Melt margarine in 12-inch pan. Fry salami and zucchini for 2 minutes over medium to high heat, stirring.
- Add eggs, sprinkle with the cheese, and cook a flat omelet, covering pan to speed the cooking. Serve at once, hot.

Truffle and Foie Gras Omelet

½ cup beef stock or broth,
    preferably unsalted
2 tablespoons cream
4 tablespoons pâté of foie gras,
    or chicken liver pâté, diced
2 small truffles, minced
2 tablespoons margarine
4 eggs, seasoned, lightly beaten
1 tablespoon cognac or brandy
    salt and pepper to taste

• Combine stock and cream in a small pan. Add foie gras and truffles; cook until almost dry over medium to high heat, stirring. Meanwhile, melt margarine in 12-inch pan and start to cook omelet over medium to high heat.

• Flame foie gras mixture with the cognac, stirring until fire dies. Season with salt and pepper.

• When omelet is nearly done, fill with the cooked foie gras mixture, fold, and finish cooking. Serve at once, hot.

NOTE: *Since this omelet filling is quite liquid, some of it may seep out of the omelet. Spoon this melted filling from the pan over the omelet when serving. You can also top a plain omelet with this filling.*

Cornmeal Pancakes *makes about 8 small pancakes*

2 tablespoons margarine,
    divided
¼ cup milk
1 egg
3 tablespoons degerminated
    cornmeal
1 tablespoon flour
¹⁄₁₆ teaspoon salt

• Purée 1 tablespoon of the margarine and the remaining ingredients in a blender on high speed until perfectly smooth.

• Melt remaining tablespoon of margarine in a 12-inch pan or griddle in two portions. Stir and then fry batter in little pancakes over medium to high heat, making two batches. Serve hot with syrup, jam, jelly, or sugar.

NOTE: *For perfectly shaped pancakes, fry individually in one or more small pans (about 4 to 6 inches in diameter).*

Quick Savory Pancakes *makes about 8 small pancakes*

2 *tablespoons margarine,*
  divided
¼ *cup milk*
1 *egg*
¼ *cup flour*
¹⁄₁₆ *teaspoon salt*

- Purée 1 tablespoon of the margarine and the remaining ingredients in a blender on high speed until perfectly smooth.

- Melt remaining tablespoon of margarine in a 12-inch pan or griddle in two portions. Stir and then fry batter in little pancakes over medium to high heat, making two batches. Serve hot with syrup, jam, jelly, or sugar.

NOTE: *For perfectly shaped pancakes, fry individually in one or more small pans (about 4 to 6 inches in diameter).*

CREAM CHEESE FILLING FOR PANCAKES

1 *teaspoon margarine*
1 *bacon strip, chopped*
¼ *cup chopped pimiento-stuffed*
  olives
½ *cup cream cheese*

- While frying pancakes, melt margarine in a small pan. Fry bacon until done over medium to high heat. Remove bacon and drain.

- Mix bacon with olives and cream cheese. Use as filling or topping for rolled or stacked pancakes.

NOTE: *This filling can be prepared while making one recipe of Quick Savory or Cornmeal Pancakes.*

HAM AND SWISS CHEESE FILLING FOR PANCAKES

1 tablespoon margarine
¼ cup minced onion
½ teaspoon caraway seeds,
    crushed in a mortar
½ cup thin, lean ham strips,
    peppered
1 tablespoon flour blended with
    ½ cup milk
½ cup thin Swiss-cheese strips

- While frying pancakes, melt margarine in a small pan. Fry onion, caraway seeds, and ham for 1 minute over medium to high heat, stirring only occasionally.

- Add the flour and milk slurry; cook to thicken, stirring.

- Mix in cheese and cook 15 seconds more, tossing. Remove from heat but continue stirring for a few seconds. Serve hot as a filling and/or topping for rolled or stacked pancakes.

NOTE: *This filling can be prepared while making one recipe of Quick Savory or Cornmeal Pancakes.*

SALMON (or Tuna) FILLING FOR PANCAKES

1 tablespoon margarine
¼ teaspoon parsley
⅛ teaspoon basil
1/16 teaspoon thyme
1 can (7 ounces) salmon or
    tuna, drained, flaked, and
    seasoned
1½ teaspoons flour blended with
    ¼ cup milk
2 tablespoons caviar (optional)

- While frying pancakes, melt margarine in a small pan. Fry herbs for a few seconds over medium to high heat, stirring.

- Add salmon and fry 2 minutes more, stirring occasionally.

- Add flour and milk slurry; cook to thicken over high heat, stirring. Use as a filling for rolled or stacked pancakes. Top with caviar and serve hot.

NOTE: *This filling can be prepared while making one recipe of Quick Savory or Cornmeal Pancakes.*

Coffee Pancakes *makes about 8 small pancakes*

2 *tablespoons margarine,*
   divided
¼ *cup milk*
1 *egg*
¼ *cup flour*
   pinch of salt
1 *tablespoon sugar*
1 *teaspoon instant coffee*

- Purée 1 tablespoon of the margarine and the remaining ingredients in a blender on high speed until perfectly smooth.

- Melt remaining tablespoon of margarine in a 12-inch pan or griddle in two portions. Stir and then fry batter in little pancakes over medium to high heat, making two batches. Serve hot with syrup, jam, jelly, sugar, and/or with whipped cream or ice cream.

NOTE: *For perfectly shaped pancakes, fry individually in one or more small pans (about 4 to 6 inches in diameter).*

Maple Pancakes *makes about 8 small pancakes*

2 *tablespoons margarine,*
   divided
¼ *cup milk*
1 *egg*
¼ *cup flour*
   pinch of salt
2 *tablespoons maple syrup*
¼ *teaspoon imitation maple*
   flavoring

- Purée 1 tablespoon of the margarine and the remaining ingredients in a blender on high speed until perfectly smooth.

- Melt remaining tablespoon of margarine in a 12-inch pan or griddle in two portions. Stir and then fry batter in little pancakes over medium to high heat, making two batches. Serve hot with syrup, jam, jelly, sugar and/or topped with whipped cream or ice cream.

NOTE: *For perfectly shaped pancakes, fry individually in one or more small pans (about 4 to 6 inches in diameter).*

SALADS
AND
VEGETABLES

Soy-Marinated Cucumber Salad

1 *chilled cucumber, peeled, split*
  lengthwise, thinly sliced
1 *tablespoon soy sauce*
2 *teaspoons cider vinegar*
  pepper to taste

- Mix all ingredients in a wide, shallow bowl and marinate for 5 minutes, tossing a few times. Serve salad in the marinating dish.

Hot Lettuce Salad

2 *tablespoons margarine*
1 *tablespoon crystallized*
  ginger, minced
1 *teaspoon anise seed, crushed*
  in a mortar
1 *small head of lettuce, cored*
  and cut into wide strips
½ *teaspoon hot pepper flakes (or*
  to taste)
1 *tablespoon cider vinegar*

- Melt margarine in 12-inch pan. Fry spices over medium to high heat for a few seconds, stirring.
- Add lettuce and fry 2 minutes more, stirring briskly. (Cover to soften lettuce if necessary.)
- Remove from heat. Add hot pepper flakes and vinegar, stirring briskly. Serve hot.

Hot Potato Salad

2 *cups water, lightly salted*
1 *tablespoon sesame seed*
2 *tablespoons cider vinegar*
1 *tablespoon dry white wine*
1 *tablespoon soy sauce*
2 *teaspoons sugar*
2 *cups thin potato slices (peeled*
  or unpeeled)
1 *tablespoon chopped chives*

- Bring water to boil in a 12-inch pan over high heat.
- Meanwhile, fry sesame seed in a small pan over medium to high heat, stirring for about 30 seconds. (No fat is needed.)
- Add vinegar, wine, soy sauce, and sugar to the small pan; mix with the sesame seed until sugar dissolves. Set aside, off heat.
- Add potatoes to boiling water and return to a boil. Cook potatoes 1 minute and drain (do not overcook). Serve potatoes hot, topped with the sesame seed mixture and sprinkled with chives.

Sweet Tart Radish Salad

1½ *cups thinly sliced radishes*
1 *tablespoon Italian olive oil*
1 *tablespoon soy sauce*
1 *tablespoon cider vinegar*
1 *teaspoon sugar*
1 *tablespoon fresh parsley*
1 *tablespoon fresh chopped chives*

- Marinate radishes in oil, soy sauce, vinegar, and sugar for 5 minutes in a wide, shallow bowl, tossing occasionally.

- Add parsley and chives; toss to distribute evenly. Serve salad in the marinating dish.

Spinach Cheese Salad

2 *tablespoons margarine*
1 *package (10 ounces) of spinach, fresh or frozen and thawed*
¼ *cup shredded cheddar cheese*
1 *tablespoon soy sauce*
1 *tablespoon cider vinegar*
pepper to taste

- Melt margarine in 10-inch pan. Fry spinach for 2 minutes over medium to high heat, stirring.

- Remove from heat. Sprinkle with cheese, soy sauce, vinegar, and pepper; toss and serve warm.

Asparagus with Yogurt

¼ *cup plain yogurt*
1 *teaspoon prepared mustard*
1 *teaspoon Worcestershire sauce*
2 *tablespoons margarine*
½ *teaspoon parsley*
1 *package (10 ounces) frozen asparagus spears, thawed and seasoned*

- Mix yogurt, mustard, and Worcestershire sauce in a small bowl or cup.

- Melt margarine in 10-inch pan. Fry parsley over medium to high heat for a few seconds, stirring. Add asparagus and fry 3 minutes more, tossing gently to cook evenly.

- Add asparagus to yogurt mixture, tossing in quickly but gently. Serve at once, hot.

Bean Sprouts with Ham

1 *tablespoon margarine*
¼ *cup chopped lean ham*
1 *can (1 pound) bean sprouts, drained*
2 *teaspoons sherry*
1 *teaspoon soy sauce (or to taste)*
  pepper to taste

- Melt margarine in 10-inch pan. Fry ham for a few seconds over medium to high heat, stirring.
- Add bean sprouts and fry 1 minute more, stirring.
- Add sherry, soy sauce, and pepper; fry 1 minute more, stirring. Serve hot.

Broccoli with Mushrooms

1 *tablespoon peanut oil*
¼ *teaspoon ginger*
1 *package (10 ounces) frozen broccoli spears, thawed, cut into bite-size pieces*
1 *can (4 ounces) sliced mushrooms, drained*
2 *tablespoons chopped scallion, including some greens*
1 *ounce Madeira*
1 *tablespoon soy sauce*
  pepper to taste

- Heat oil in 10-inch pan. Fry ginger for a few seconds over medium to high heat, stirring.
- Add broccoli, mushrooms, and scallion; fry 4 minutes more, stirring continuously but gently.
- Add Madeira, soy sauce, and pepper to taste; fry 30 seconds more, stirring. Serve hot.

Brussels Sprouts with Cheese

1 *tablespoon margarine*
2 *tablespoons minced onion*
2 *tablespoons minced celery*
¼ *cup nuts (cashews, peanuts, or almonds)*
1 *package (10 ounces) frozen brussels sprouts, thawed and halved lengthwise*
  salt and pepper to taste
½ *cup shredded cheddar cheese (or to taste)*

- Melt margarine in 10-inch pan. Fry onion and celery for 30 seconds over medium to high heat, stirring.
- Add nuts and brussels sprouts; season with salt and pepper and fry 3 minutes more, stirring.
- Add cheese and toss until melted. Serve hot.

Cabbage with Ham

2 tablespoons margarine
½ teaspoon parsley
¼ teaspoon oregano
⅛ teaspoon thyme
½ small head of cabbage, cored, cut into wide strips (discard thick leaf ribs)
¼ cup chopped lean ham
1 ounce dry white wine
1 tablespoon soy sauce
  pepper to taste

• Melt margarine in 12-inch pan. Fry herbs over medium to high heat for a few seconds, stirring.

• Add cabbage, ham, wine, soy sauce, and pepper; cover and fry 5 minutes more, tossing occasionally. Serve hot.

Cauliflower with Cashews

2 tablespoons margarine
½ cup cashew nuts
1 package (10 ounces) frozen cauliflower, thawed, cut into bite-size pieces
  salt, pepper, and grated nutmeg to taste
½ cup heavy cream

• Melt margarine in 10-inch pan. Fry cashews for 1 minute over medium to high heat, stirring.

• Add cauliflower and fry 2 minutes more, stirring briskly but gently with a spatula (to prevent nuts from scorching).

• Season with salt, pepper, and grated nutmeg. Add cream and cook for 1 minute more, stirring gently. Serve hot.

Stir-Fried Corn with Scallions

2 tablespoons margarine
½ teaspoon cumin
½ teaspoon chili powder
⅛ teaspoon ground bay leaf
1½ cups corn kernels
  salt and pepper to taste
3 scallions, cut into thin strips

• Melt margarine in 12-inch pan. Fry spices over medium to high heat for a few seconds, stirring.

• Add corn and fry 2 minutes more, stirring briskly.

• Season with salt and pepper. Add scallions and fry 1 minute more, stirring. Serve hot.

Creamed Corn

1 tablespoon margarine
¼ cup chopped onion
1 package (10 ounces) frozen corn, thawed
¼ cup chicken stock or broth, preferably unsalted
  salt, pepper, and grated nutmeg to taste
¼ cup heavy cream
1 teaspoon flour blended with ¼ cup milk

- Melt margarine in 10-inch pan. Fry onion for 30 seconds over medium to high heat, stirring.

- Add corn and fry 1 minute more, stirring. Add chicken stock, salt, pepper, and grated nutmeg; fry 30 seconds, stirring.

- Add cream and fry 1 minute more, stirring. Blend in flour and milk slurry to thicken. Serve hot.

Sweet and Sour Cucumbers

1 tablespoon vegetable oil
1 cucumber, peeled, halved lengthwise (seeded if desired), and thinly sliced
1 teaspoon soy sauce (or to taste)
1½ tablespoons cider vinegar blended with 1 tablespoon sugar
  white pepper to taste
1 very small hot pepper, seeded and chopped (optional)

- Heat oil in 10-inch pan. Fry cucumber for 2 minutes over medium to high heat, stirring.

- Add soy sauce, vinegar mixture, and white pepper; fry 2 minutes more, stirring. Serve hot, or at room temperature, garnished with chopped hot pepper if desired.

Eggplant with Shrimp

2 *tablespoons margarine*
1 *garlic clove, minced*
¼ *teaspoon ginger*
2 *cups chopped eggplant*
2 *scallions, cut into strips*
½ *cup tiny shrimp, cleaned*
1 *tablespoon soy sauce*
1 *tablespoon Madeira*
  pepper to taste

- Melt margarine in 10-inch pan. Fry garlic and ginger for a few seconds over medium to high heat, stirring.
- Add eggplant and fry 3 minutes more, covered.
- Add scallions and shrimp; fry 1 minute, stirring.
- Add soy sauce, Madeira, and pepper; fry 1 minute, stirring. Serve hot.

Spicy Fruit

¼ *cup chopped figs*
¼ *cup chopped dates*
½ *cup dry white wine*
1½ *tablespoons margarine*
⅛ *teaspoon cinnamon*
1⁄16 *teaspoon nutmeg*
  dash of ground cloves
1½ *cups peeled, cored, sliced*
  apples

- Simmer figs and dates in wine for 3 minutes in a small pot over medium to high heat.
- Meanwhile, melt margarine in 10-inch pan. Fry spices for a few seconds over medium to high heat, stirring. Add apples and fry 3 minutes more, stirring gently.
- Add plumped figs and dates, and any remaining wine, to the apples; cook 1 minute more, tossing gently. Serve hot.

Green Peppers with Bean Sprouts

2 *tablespoons peanut oil*
2 *green peppers, cut into 1-inch*
  squares
1 *tablespoon soy sauce*
1 *cup bean sprouts*
¼ *cup tomato sauce, hot*

- Heat oil in 12-inch pan. Fry peppers for 3 minutes over medium to high heat, covered, stirring about every 15 seconds.
- Add soy sauce and blend in quickly. Add bean sprouts and fry 1 minute, covered, stirring about every 15 seconds.
- Add tomato sauce and fry 30 seconds, stirring. Serve hot.

Lettuce with Bamboo Shoots and Water Chestnuts

2 *tablespoons margarine*
1 *garlic clove, minced*
¼ *teaspoon parsley*
⅛ *teaspoon basil*
3 *cups lettuce strips, half-inch wide (do not use thick leaves)*
½ *(8-ounce) can bamboo shoots, drained and slivered*
½ *(8-ounce) can water chestnuts, drained and thinly sliced*
1 *scallion, cut into strips*
1 *tablespoon soy sauce*
1 *tablespoon sherry*
  pepper to taste

- Melt margarine in 12-inch pan. Fry garlic and herbs for a few seconds over medium to high heat, stirring.

- Add lettuce, bamboo shoots, and water chestnuts; fry 3 minutes more, covered, stirring occasionally until lettuce wilts slightly.

- Add scallion and fry 30 seconds more, stirring.

- Add soy sauce, sherry, and pepper; fry 30 seconds more, stirring. Serve hot.

Spicy Mushrooms

3 *tablespoons margarine*
1 *small onion, thinly sliced*
1 *garlic clove, minced*
¼ *teaspoon ginger*
¼ *teaspoon cumin*
⅛ *teaspoon turmeric*
⅛ *teaspoon cinnamon*
1/16 *teaspoon ground cloves*
1½ *cups thinly sliced mushrooms*
  pepper to taste
½ *tablespoon soy sauce*
1 *tablespoon Madeira*

- Melt margarine in 10-inch pan. Fry onion, garlic, and spices for 1 minute over medium to high heat, stirring briskly.

- Add mushrooms and fry 2 minutes more, stirring. Season with pepper.

- Add soy sauce and Madeira; fry 1 minute, stirring. Serve hot.

Mustard Greens with Pork

1½ *tablespoons margarine*
1 *garlic clove, minced*
¼ *pound lean ground pork*
1 *package (10 ounces) frozen*
  mustard greens, thawed
1 *tablespoon soy sauce*
1 *tablespoon Madeira*
½ *cup chicken stock or broth,*
  preferably unsalted
  pepper to taste
1 *tablespoon cornstarch*
  blended with 1 tablespoon
  Madeira

- Melt margarine in 10-inch pan. Fry garlic for a few seconds over medium to high heat, stirring.

- Add pork and fry 2 minutes more, stirring briskly. Add mustard greens and fry 3 minutes, stirring.

- Add soy sauce, Madeira, stock, and pepper; mix together well.

- Blend in cornstarch and Madeira slurry to thicken. Serve hot.

Peas with Prosciutto

1 *tablespoon margarine*
¼ *teaspoon parsley*
⅛ *teaspoon tarragon*
¼ *cup minced onion*
1 *garlic clove, minced*
2 *slices lean prosciutto, chopped*
1 *package (10 ounces) frozen*
  peas, thawed
  salt and pepper to taste

- Melt margarine in 10-inch pan. Fry herbs, onion, garlic, and prosciutto for 30 seconds over medium to high heat, stirring.

- Add peas and salt and pepper; fry 3 minutes more, stirring. Serve hot.

Herbed Potatoes

3 tablespoons margarine
½ teaspoon parsley
¼ teaspoon basil
⅛ teaspoon oregano
¼ cup minced onion
2 cups finely minced potatoes
 salt and pepper to taste
¼ cup sour cream (optional)
 chopped fresh parsley and/or
 chives

- Melt margarine in 12-inch pan. Fry herbs and onion for a few seconds over medium to low heat, stirring.

- Add potatoes, salt, and pepper; cook covered for 5 minutes, stirring occasionally.

- Mix in sour cream if desired; sprinkle with fresh parsley and/or chives and serve hot.

Snow Peas, Mushrooms, and Ham

1 tablespoon margarine
1 garlic clove, minced
1 scallion, chopped
¼ cup chopped lean ham
1 can (4 ounces) sliced
 mushrooms, drained
1 package (6 ounces) frozen
 snow peas, thawed
 salt and pepper to taste

- Melt margarine in 10-inch pan. Fry garlic and scallion for a few seconds over medium to high heat, stirring.

- Add ham and mushrooms; fry 1 minute more, stirring.

- Add snow peas, salt, and pepper; fry 2 minutes, stirring. Serve hot.

Spiced Tomatoes

2 tablespoons margarine
1 teaspoon parsley
1 teaspoon basil
½ teaspoon oregano
¼ teaspoon ground bay leaf
1/16 teaspoon ground cloves
3 tomatoes, thickly sliced, and
 well-seasoned

- Melt margarine in 12-inch pan. Fry spices over medium to high heat for a few seconds, stirring.

- Add tomatoes and fry 4 minutes more, turning a few times during cooking. Serve hot.

Spinach with Apple

2 *tablespoons peanut oil*
2 *tablespoons sesame seed*
¼ *teaspoon ginger*
1 *package (10 ounces) of spinach, fresh or frozen and thawed*
1 *tablespoon soy sauce*
1 *apple, peeled, cored, and thinly sliced*

• Heat oil in 10-inch pan. Fry sesame seed and ginger over medium to high heat for a few seconds, stirring.

• Add spinach and fry 1 minute more, stirring briskly. Add soy sauce and blend quickly.

• Lower heat and add apple. Fry 1 minutes more, covered, tossing a few times. Serve hot.

Squash with Scallions

1 *tablespoon margarine*
1 *garlic clove, minced*
½ *pound yellow summer squash, halved lengthwise and thinly sliced*
1 *scallion, chopped*
salt and pepper to taste
2 *tablespoons water*

• Melt margarine in 10-inch pan. Fry garlic for a few seconds over medium to high heat, stirring.

• Add squash, scallion, salt, and pepper; fry 1 minute more, stirring.

• Add water, cover, and cook 4 minutes. Serve hot.

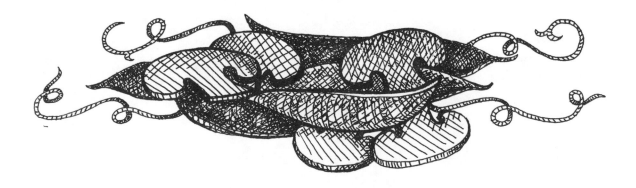

Stir-Fried Yams with Port

3 tablespoons margarine
½ teaspoon parsley
½ teaspoon chopped chives
2 cups finely chopped yams
    salt and pepper to taste
1 ounce tawny port wine

- Melt margarine in 12-inch pan. Fry parsley and chives over medium to high heat for a few seconds, stirring.

- Add yams and fry 4 minutes more, stirring briskly. Season with salt and pepper.

- Add port wine and blend in quickly. Serve hot.

Sweet and Sour Zucchini

2 tablespoons margarine
1 garlic clove, minced
½ cup very thinly sliced onion
¼ cup chopped tomato
2 cups thinly sliced zucchini,
    peppered
¼ cup hot chicken stock or
    broth, preferably unsalted
1 tablespoon soy sauce
1 tablespoon sugar
1 tablespoon cider vinegar

- Melt margarine in 10-inch pan. Fry garlic, onion, and tomato over medium to high heat for a few seconds, stirring.

- Add zucchini and stock; cook 5 minutes, covered, over medium to high heat.

- Add soy sauce, sugar, and vinegar; blend in quickly. Serve hot.

RICE AND PASTA

Almond Rice

¾ cup well-seasoned, strongly flavored beef or chicken stock or broth
¾ cup quick-cooking rice
½ cup slivered, blanched almonds

• Boil stock in a small pot. Stir in rice, cover tightly, and set aside for 5 minutes.

• Meanwhile, fry and stir almonds in a 10-inch pan over medium to high heat until lightly browned, about 4 minutes. Remove from pan.

• When rice is done, toss with almonds; serve hot.

Rice with Beef and Bean Sprouts

¾ cup well-seasoned, strongly flavored beef stock or broth
¾ cup quick-cooking rice
1½ tablespoons margarine
⅛ teaspoon ginger
¼ teaspoon parsley
⅛ teaspoon basil
2 tablespoons minced onion
2 garlic cloves, minced
½ pound small, thin beef strips, seasoned
1 tablespoon Madeira
1 cup bean sprouts

• Boil stock in a small pot. Stir in rice, cover tightly, and set aside for 5 minutes.

• Meanwhile, melt margarine in 10-inch pan. Fry ginger and herbs for a few seconds over medium to high heat, stirring. Add onion and garlic and fry 30 seconds more, stirring. Add beef and fry 2 minutes, stirring. Add Madeira and fry 30 seconds, stirring. Add bean sprouts and fry 1 minute more, stirring.

• When rice is done, add to pan and stir well over heat for a few seconds. Serve hot. (Or, serve rice topped with the beef mixture.)

Rice with Cheese

¾ cup well-seasoned, strongly flavored chicken stock or broth
¾ cup quick-cooking rice
¾ cup shredded cheddar cheese

• Boil stock in a small pot. Stir in rice, cover tightly, and set aside for 5 minutes or as long as called for in package directions.

• When rice is done, toss immediately with cheese and serve hot.

Fried Rice

¾ *cup well-seasoned, strongly flavored beef stock or broth*
¾ *cup quick-cooking rice*
2 *tablespoons margarine*
¼ *teaspoon ginger*
½ *cup thinly sliced onion*
1 *garlic clove, minced*
½ *cup slivered lean ham*
½ *cup very small shrimp, shelled and cleaned*
½ *cup frozen peas, thawed*
1 *scallion, cut into strips*
1 *tablespoon soy sauce mixed with 1 tablespoon sherry*
pepper to taste

- Boil stock in a small pot. Stir in rice, cover tightly, and set aside for 5 minutes or as long as called for in package directions.
- Meanwhile, melt margarine in 10-inch pan. Fry ginger, onion, and garlic for 30 seconds over medium to high heat, stirring. Add ham, shrimp, peas, and scallion; fry 3 minutes more, stirring. Add soy sauce mixture and pepper; mix in well. Set aside and keep hot.
- When rice is done, add to pan. Stir in well and serve hot.

Giblet Rice

¾ *cup well-seasoned, strongly flavored chicken stock or broth*
¾ *cup quick-cooking rice*
2 *tablespoons margarine*
2 *chicken livers, cut into small pieces*
2 *chicken gizzards, trimmed of membranes and minced*
2 *chicken hearts, chopped*
¼ *cup chopped onion*
1 *garlic clove, minced*
¼ *teaspoon parsley*
⅛ *teaspoon tarragon*
salt and pepper to taste
1 *can (4 ounces) sliced mushrooms, drained*

- Boil stock in a small pot. Stir in rice, cover tightly, and set aside for 5 minutes or as long as called for in package directions.
- Meanwhile, melt margarine in 10-inch pan. Fry giblets for 3 minutes over medium to high heat, stirring. Add onion, garlic, herbs, salt, and pepper; fry 30 seconds more, stirring. Add mushrooms and fry 1½ minutes more, stirring.
- When rice is done, toss with giblets and serve hot.

NOTE: *This rice dish is excellent as a pan stuffing to accompany any fowl.*

Rice Imperial

¾ cup milk mixed with
    1 tablespoon sugar and
    ¼ teaspoon vanilla
    extract
¾ cup quick-cooking rice
1 tablespoon margarine
4 canned pear halves (syrup-
    packed), drained, syrup
    reserved
1 ounce rum
¼ cup strained apricot jam

- Bring milk mixture just to a boil in a small pot. Stir in rice, cover tightly, and set aside for 5 minutes or as long as called for in package directions.

- Meanwhile, melt margarine in a small pan. Fry pear halves for 2 minutes over medium to low heat. Flame pears with rum, stirring gently until fire dies. Add apricot jam and simmer gently 1 minute, tossing carefully to coat pears. Add 1 tablespoon of reserved pear syrup to make a light sauce. remove from heat.

- When rice is done, serve hot, topped with pears and sauce.

Rice with Mushrooms

¾ cup well-seasoned, strongly
    flavored beef stock or broth
¾ cup quick-cooking rice
2 tablespoons margarine
¼ teaspoon parsley
⅛ teaspoon tarragon
2 tablespoons minced onion
1 garlic clove, minced
2 tablespoons chopped lean
    ham (optional)
¼ pound mushrooms, sliced, or
    1 can (4 ounces), drained
salt and pepper to taste

- Boil stock in a small pot. Stir in rice, cover tightly, and set aside for 5 minutes or as long as called for in package directions.

- Meanwhile, melt margarine in 10-inch pan. Fry remaining ingredients for 3 minutes over medium to high heat, stirring.

- When rice is done, toss with mushroom mixture in pan and serve hot.

Rice with Onions

¾ cup well-seasoned, strongly
   flavored beef stock or
   broth
¾ cup quick-cooking rice
1½ tablespoons margarine
1 cup sliced onions, slices
   halved and separated into
   half-rings
   salt and pepper to taste

- Boil stock in a small pot. Stir in rice, cover tightly, and set aside for 5 minutes.
- Meanwhile, melt margarine in 10-inch pan. Fry onions and salt and pepper for 4 minutes over medium to high heat, stirring.
- When rice is done, toss with onions in pan and serve hot.

Quick Paella

¾ cup well-seasoned, strongly
   flavored chicken stock or
   broth
¼ teaspoon turmeric
¾ cup quick-cooking rice
3 tablespoons margarine
½ cup chicken breast meat, cut
   into ⅛-inch-thick slices
¼ cup thinly sliced green pepper
¼ cup thinly sliced onion
1 garlic clove, minced
¼ pound shrimp, shelled and
   cleaned (cut into bite-size
   pieces if desired)
6 clams or mussels, shucked,
   juices reserved (or 6 canned
   clams)
½ cup frozen peas, thawed
   salt and pepper to taste
½ cup pimiento slices

- Boil stock in a small pot. Stir in turmeric and then rice, cover tightly, and set aside for 5 minutes or as long as called for in package directions.
- Meanwhile, melt margarine in 12-inch pan. Fry chicken, green pepper, onion, and garlic for 2 minutes over medium to high heat, stirring. Add shrimp, clams and their juices, peas, salt, and pepper; fry 2 minutes more, stirring. Add pimientos and fry 1 minute, tossing gently.
- When rice is done, serve hot, topped with the chicken mixture.

NOTE: If you find it difficult to shuck fresh clams, you can scrub them well and then cook them whole with the other ingredients, shucking later after they're done. Allow for longer cooking time and cover the pan as much as possible to steam the clams.

Rice with Paprika Sauce

¾ *cup well-seasoned, strongly flavored chicken stock or broth*
¾ *cup quick-cooking rice*
2 *teaspoons margarine*
¼ *cup minced onion*
1½ *teaspoons paprika*
½ *cup sour cream*
salt to taste

- Boil stock in a small pot. Stir in rice, cover tightly, and set aside for 5 minutes or as long as called for in package directions.

- Meanwhile, melt margarine in a small pan. Fry onion for 2 minutes over medium to high heat, stirring. Add paprika, sour cream, and salt; blend in well. Remove from heat and keep hot.

- When rice is done, toss with paprika sauce and serve hot.

Rice with Peppers

¾ *cup well-seasoned, strongly flavored chicken stock or broth*
¾ *cup quick-cooking rice*
2 *tablespoons margarine*
¼ *teaspoon parsley*
1 *green pepper, seeded, cut into bite-size pieces*
1 *red pepper (sweet), seeded, cut into bite-size pieces*

- Boil stock in a small pot. Stir in rice, cover tightly, and set aside for 5 minutes or as long as called for in package directions.

- Meanwhile, melt margarine in 10-inch pan. Fry parsley and peppers for 3 minutes over medium to high heat, stirring.

- When rice is done, toss in pan with peppers and serve hot.

Quick Pilaf

¾ *cup well-seasoned, strongly flavored chicken stock or broth*
¾ *cup quick-cooking rice*
2 *tablespoons margarine*
¼ *pound lean lamb, cut into small ⅛-inch-thick slices*
¼ *cup pine nuts*
¼ *cup thinly sliced onion*
salt and pepper to taste

- Boil stock in a small pot. Stir in rice, cover tightly, and set aside for 5 minutes or as long as called for in package directions.

- Meanwhile, melt margarine in 10-inch pan. Fry lamb, pine nuts, onion, salt, and pepper for 4 minutes over medium to high heat, stirring.

- When rice is done, toss in pan with lamb mixture and serve hot.

Rice Provençale

¾ *cup well-seasoned, strongly flavored chicken stock or broth*
¾ *cup quick-cooking rice*
1 *tablespoon margarine*
1 *tablespoon Italian olive oil*
½ *teaspoon parsley*
¼ *teaspoon basil*
⅛ *teaspoon thyme*
½ *cup chopped onion*
½ *cup finely sliced green pepper*
1 *tomato, chopped*
  salt and pepper to taste
4 *pitted green olives, halved*
4 *pitted black olives, halved*
2 *teaspoons capers*
4 *anchovy fillets*

• Boil stock in a small pot. Stir in rice, cover tightly, and set aside for 5 minutes or as long as called for in package directions.

• Meanwhile, heat margarine and oil in 10-inch pan. Fry herbs, onion, and green pepper for 2 minutes over medium to high heat, stirring. Add the tomato, salt, and pepper; fry 3 minutes more, stirring.

• When rice is done, toss with tomato mixture in pan. Serve hot, garnished with the olives, capers, and anchovies.

Rice with Sausage

¾ *cup well-seasoned, strongly flavored chicken stock or broth*
¾ *cup quick-cooking rice*
1 *tablespoon margarine*
¼ *pound sausage (or mixed sausages), thinly sliced*
2 *scallions, cut into strips*
1 *tablespoon soy sauce*

• Boil stock in a small pot. Stir in rice, cover tightly, and set aside for 5 minutes or as long as called for in package directions.

• Meanwhile, melt margarine in 10-inch pan. Fry sausage for 2 minutes over medium to high heat, stirring. Add scallions and fry 3 minutes more, stirring. Drain off excess fat. Remove from heat and add soy sauce.

• When rice is done, add to pan and toss with sausage and scallions. Serve hot.

Shrimp Curry

¾ cup well-seasoned, strongly
　　flavored chicken stock or
　　broth
¾ cup quick-cooking rice
2 tablespoons margarine
½ tablespoon curry powder
½ small onion, minced
1 tablespoon raisins
½ pound shrimp, shelled and
　　cleaned
2 cups thin lettuce strips
　　salt and pepper to taste
1 teaspoon cornstarch blended
　　with ¼ cup chicken stock

- Boil stock in a small pot. Stir in rice, cover tightly, and set aside for 5 minutes or as long as called for in package directions.

- Meanwhile, melt margarine in 10-inch pan. Fry curry powder, onion, and raisins for 30 seconds over medium to high heat, stirring. Add shrimp and fry just until it turns pink, stirring about 2 minutes. Add lettuce, salt, and pepper; fry 2 minutes over lower heat, stirring. Blend in cornstarch and stock slurry to thicken over higher heat, stirring constantly.

- When rice is done, toss with shrimp mixture in pan and serve hot.

Rice with Spicy Fruit

1 cup well-seasoned, strongly
　　flavored chicken stock or
　　broth
¾ cup quick-cooking rice
¼ cup flaked coconut
1 tablespoon margarine
⅛ teaspoon ginger
⅛ teaspoon coriander
⅛ teaspoon cinnamon
1/16 teaspoon nutmeg
　　dash of ground cloves
¼ cup sliced peaches
¼ cup sliced apricots
¼ cup sliced firm bananas
¼ cup pine nuts

- Boil stock in a small pot. Stir in rice and coconut, cover tightly, and set aside for 5 minutes.

- Meanwhile, melt margarine in 10-inch pan. Fry spices for a few seconds over medium to low heat, stirring. Add fruits and pine nuts. Simmer 3 minutes, first stirring in gently to mix with spices, then tossing gently a few times.

- When coconut-rice mixture is done, toss with fruits and nuts. Serve hot.

Tomato Rice

¾ cup well-seasoned tomato
   juice
¾ cup quick-cooking rice
1 tablespoon margarine
¼ teaspoon parsley
⅛ teaspoon oregano
⅛ teaspoon basil
¼ cup chopped onion
2 garlic cloves, minced
1 cup coarsely chopped
   tomatoes and their juices
   salt and pepper to taste

• Boil tomato juice in a small pot. Stir in rice, cover tightly, and set aside for 5 minutes or as long as called for in package directions.

• Meanwhile, melt margarine in 10-inch pan. Fry herbs, onion, and garlic for 30 seconds over medium to high heat, stirring. Add tomatoes and their juices, salt, and pepper; fry 2 minutes more, stirring a few times.

• When rice is done, toss in pan with tomato mixture and serve hot.

Rice with Tuna

¾ cup well-seasoned, strongly
   flavored chicken stock or
   broth
¾ cup quick-cooking rice
1 tablespoon margarine
¼ cup chopped onion
1 garlic clove, minced
2 tablespoons lean chopped
   ham
1 can (7 ounces) tuna, drained
   and flaked
   salt and pepper to taste
½ cup tomato sauce

• Boil stock in a small pot. Stir in rice, cover tightly, and set aside for 5 minutes.

• Meanwhile, melt margarine in 10-inch pan. Fry onion and garlic for 1 minute over medium to high heat, stirring. Add ham, tuna, salt, and pepper; fry 2 minutes more, stirring. Add tomato sauce and heat through.

• When rice is done, toss with tuna mixture in pan and serve hot.

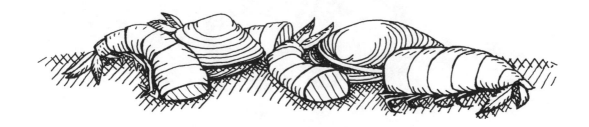

Rice with Vegetables

¾ *cup well-seasoned, strongly flavored chicken stock or broth*
¾ *cup quick-cooking rice*
1½ *tablespoons margarine*
½ *package frozen mixed vegetables, thawed*
    salt and pepper to taste

- Boil stock in a small pot. Stir in rice, cover tightly, and set aside for 5 minutes.

- Meanwhile, melt margarine in 10-inch pan. Fry vegetables, salt, and pepper for 4 minutes over medium to high heat, stirring.

- When rice is done, toss with vegetables in pan and serve hot.

Venetian Rice

¾ *cup well-seasoned, strongly flavored chicken stock or broth*
¾ *cup quick-cooking rice*
1 *tablespoon margarine*
¼ *cup minced onion*
½ *cup lean ham cubes*
½ *cup frozen peas, thawed*
   salt and pepper to taste
¼ *cup grated Parmesan cheese*

- Boil stock in a small pot. Stir in rice, cover tightly, and set aside for 5 minutes or as long as called for in package directions.

- Meanwhile, melt margarine in 10-inch pan. Fry onion, ham, peas, salt, and pepper for 3 minutes over medium to high heat, stirring. Set aside and keep hot.

- When rice is done, toss with ham mixture and grated cheese. Serve hot.

Linguini with Peas and Scallions

⅜ pound linguini, cooked to desired tenderness in salted water, drained, hot
1 tablespoon margarine
¼ teaspoon parsley
⅛ teaspoon basil
1/16 teaspoon oregano
½ package frozen peas, thawed
2 scallions, cut into strips
¼ cup chicken stock or broth blended with 2 tablespoons tomato paste
salt and pepper to taste
grated Parmesan cheese

• While linguini cooks, melt margarine in small pan. Fry herbs, peas, and scallions for 3 minutes over medium to high heat, stirring. Add stock mixture, salt, and pepper; heat through, mixing in well. Remove from heat and keep hot.

• When linguini is done, toss with pea mixture and serve hot, with grated cheese on the side.

Spaghetti with Anchovies

⅜ pound spaghetti, cooked to desired tenderness in salted water, drained, and hot
2 tablespoons Italian olive oil
½ teaspoon parsley
¼ teaspoon rosemary
several fresh celery leaves, chopped
¼ cup chopped onion
4 to 6 anchovy fillets, drained well on paper towels, chopped
2 teaspoons tomato sauce
1 tablespoon dry white wine
pepper to taste
grated Parmesan cheese

• While spaghetti cooks, heat oil in a small pan. Fry herbs, celery leaves, and onion for 1 minute over medium to high heat, stirring. Add anchovies and fry 30 seconds more, stirring. Blend in tomato sauce and wine, then remove mixture from heat and keep hot.

• When spaghetti is done, toss with anchovy mixture and add pepper. Serve hot with grated Parmesan cheese.

Garlic Spaghetti

⅜ *pound spaghetti, cooked to desired tenderness in salted water, drained, and hot*
3 *tablespoons margarine*
4 *garlic cloves, crushed (or to taste)*
  pepper to taste
  chopped fresh parsley and/or chives
  grated Parmesan cheese

- While spaghetti cooks, melt margarine in a small pan. Fry garlic until lightly browned over medium to high heat, about 3 minutes. Discard garlic and set margarine off heat. Keep hot.
- When spaghetti is done, toss with garlic-flavored margarine and pepper. Serve hot, garnished with parsley and/or chives and cheese to taste.

Spaghetti with Meat Sauce

⅜ *pound spaghetti, cooked to desired tenderness in salted water, drained, and hot*
1 *tablespoon margarine*
¼ *pound lean ground beef*
¼ *pound lean ground pork*
2 *tablespoons chopped lean ham*
2 *tablespoons chopped onion*
1 *tablespoon chopped celery leaves*
  salt and pepper to taste
2 *tablespoons dry red wine*
½ *cup tomato sauce*
  grated Parmesan cheese

- While spaghetti cooks, melt margarine in 10-inch pan. Fry beef, pork, ham, onion, celery, salt, and pepper for 3 minutes over medium to high heat, stirring. Add wine and tomato sauce; simmer a few seconds more, stirring. Remove from heat and keep hot.
- When spaghetti is done, toss with meat sauce and serve hot, with grated cheese.

Spaghetti with Italian Sausage

⅜ *pound spaghetti, cooked to desired tenderness in salted water, drained, and hot*
1 *tablespoon margarine*
½ *pound Italian sausage (sweet or hot, or half of each), thinly sliced*
2 *garlic cloves, minced (optional)*
½ *cup tomato sauce*
2 *tablespoons heavy cream grated Parmesan cheese*

- While spaghetti cooks, melt margarine in 10-inch pan. Fry sausage and garlic for 4½ minutes over medium to high heat, stirring. Drain off excess fat. Add tomato sauce and cream; cook 30 seconds more, stirring.

- When spaghetti is done, toss with sauce and serve hot, with grated cheese.

Spaghetti with White Clam Sauce

⅜ *pound spaghetti, cooked to desired tenderness in salted water, drained, and hot*
2 *tablespoons margarine*
1 *garlic clove, minced*
¼ *teaspoon parsley*
⅛ *teaspoon basil*
12 *fresh cherrystone clams, shucked, chopped, juices reserved (or one 6½-ounce can minced clams and the juices)*
  pepper to taste
1 *teaspoon flour blended with 2 tablespoons dry white wine grated Parmesan cheese*

- While spaghetti cooks, melt margarine in 10-inch pan. Fry garlic, herbs, clams, and pepper for 2 minutes over medium to high heat, stirring. Add clam juice and the flour and wine slurry; mix well and cook to thicken, stirring. Set off heat and keep hot.

- When spaghetti is done, toss with clam sauce and serve hot, with grated cheese.

Vermicelli with Tomato Sauce

⅜ pound vermicelli, cooked to
    desired tenderness in salted
    water, drained, and hot
1 tablespoon margarine
¼ teaspoon parsley
⅛ teaspoon basil
1/16 teaspoon oregano
¼ cup very thinly sliced green
    pepper
¼ cup very thinly sliced onion
1 garlic clove, minced
1 cup chopped tomatoes
    salt and pepper to taste
2 teaspoons tomato paste
    grated Parmesan cheese

- While vermicelli cooks, melt margarine in 10-inch pan. Fry herbs, green pepper, onion, and garlic for 30 seconds over medium to high heat, stirring. Add tomatoes, salt, and pepper; fry 4 minutes more, stirring and mashing tomatoes with a fork. Blend in tomato paste; set off heat and keep hot.

- When vermicelli is done, toss with tomato sauce and serve hot, with grated cheese.

Vermicelli with Tuna Sauce

⅜ pound vermicelli, cooked to
    desired tenderness in salted
    water, drained, and hot
2 tablespoons margarine
1 garlic clove, minced
½ cup sliced mushrooms
1 can (7 ounces) tuna fish,
    drained and flaked
2 tablespoons tomato purée
    salt and pepper to taste
    grated Parmesan cheese

- While vermicelli cooks, melt margarine in small pan. Fry garlic for a few seconds over medium to high heat, stirring. Add mushrooms and fry 2 minutes more, stirring. Add tuna and fry 1 minute more, stirring. Mix in tomato purée and salt and pepper. Set off heat and keep hot.

- When vermicelli is done, toss with tuna sauce. Serve hot, with grated cheese.

BEEF AND LIVER

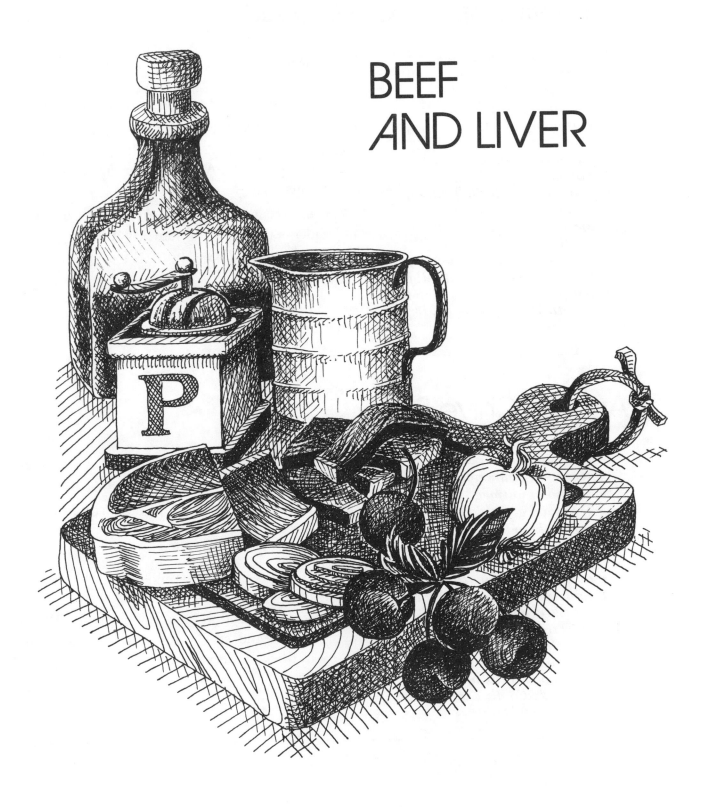

Beef with Apple Cider Sauce

3 tablespoons margarine
¼ teaspoon cinnamon
⅛ teaspoon nutmeg
¹⁄₁₆ teaspoon ground cloves
⅛ teaspoon fennel seed, crushed in a mortar
¼ cup minced onion
1 pound lean beef, cut into small ⅛-inch-thick slices, seasoned
1 apple, peeled, cored, thinly sliced
½ cup cider or apple juice, hot
2 teaspoons red currant jelly
2 teaspoons cornstarch blended with 1 tablespoon cold cider

• Melt margarine in 12-inch pan. Fry spices over medium to high heat for a few seconds, stirring. Add onion and fry 30 seconds, stirring briskly.

• Add beef and fry 2 minutes, stirring and turning pieces to cook evenly. Add apple and fry 1 minute, stirring gently. Add cider and fry 1 minute, stirring gently.

• Blend in jelly quickly but gently. Add cornstarch and cider slurry; stir in quickly but gently to blend and thicken. Serve hot.

Apricot Chive Beef

3 tablespoons margarine
¼ teaspoon cinnamon
⅛ teaspoon nutmeg
¹⁄₁₆ teaspoon ground cloves
1 pound lean beef, cut into small ⅛-inch-thick slices, seasoned
1 ounce brandy, warm
1 tablespoon chopped chives or green onion tops
1½ cups thinly sliced apricots
½ cup chicken stock or broth, preferably unsalted, hot
2 teaspoons cornstarch blended with 1 tablespoon cold chicken stock

• Melt margarine in 12-inch pan. Fry spices over medium to high heat for a few seconds, stirring.

• Add beef and fry 3 minutes more, stirring briskly and turning pieces to cook evenly. Flame with brandy, stirring until fire dies.

• Blend in chives quickly. Add apricots and fry 30 seconds more, stirring gently.

• Add stock and blend in quickly but gently. Blend in cornstarch and stock slurry; stir quickly but gently to thicken. Serve hot.

Beef, Beer, and Onions

2 tablespoons margarine
1 garlic clove, minced
½ teaspoon parsley
¼ teaspoon oregano
⅛ teaspoon ground bay leaf
1 cup minced onion
1 pound lean beef, cut into
   small ⅛-inch-thick slices,
   seasoned
½ cup beer, hot
1 teaspoon brown sugar
2 teaspoons cider vinegar
2 teaspoons cornstarch blended
   with 1 tablespoon cold beer

• Melt margarine in 12-inch pan. Fry garlic and herbs over medium to high heat for a few seconds, stirring. Add onion and fry 1 minute more, stirring briskly.

• Add beef and fry 2 minutes, stirring and turning pieces to cook evenly. Add beer and fry 30 seconds more, stirring.

• Blend in sugar quickly. Add vinegar and blend in quickly. Add cornstarch and beer slurry; stir in briskly to blend and thicken. Serve hot.

Stir-Fried Beef Bourguignon

2 tablespoons margarine
1 garlic clove, minced
¼ teaspoon thyme
⅛ teaspoon ground bay leaf
½ carrot, shaved with a potato
   peeler
¼ cup minced onion
1 pound lean beef, cut into
   small ⅛-inch-thick slices,
   seasoned
¼ cup thin, lean ham strips
¼ cup dry red wine, hot
¼ cup beef stock or broth,
   preferably unsalted, hot
1 teaspoon tomato paste
2 teaspoons cornstarch blended
   with 1 tablespoon cold beef
   stock

• Melt margarine in 12-inch pan. Fry garlic and herbs over medium to high heat for a few seconds, stirring.

• Add carrot and onion; fry 1 minute more, stirring briskly. Add beef and ham and fry 2 minutes, stirring and turning pieces to cook evenly. Add wine and stock and fry 30 seconds more, stirring.

• Add tomato paste and blend in quickly. Add cornstarch and stock slurry; stir in briskly to blend and thicken. Serve hot.

Stir-Fried Beef with Cheese

2 *tablespoons margarine*
1 *pound lean beef, cut into small ⅛-inch-thick slices, peppered*
2 *scallions, cut into thin strips*
1 *tablespoon soy sauce*
½ *cup grated Swiss cheese (or to taste)*

- Melt margarine in 10-inch pan. Fry beef for 2 minutes over medium to high heat, stirring briskly and turning pieces to cook evenly.
- Add scallions and soy sauce; fry 1 minute more, stirring. Add cheese and toss together to blend and melt. Serve hot.

Cherry Beef

2 *tablespoons margarine*
1 *pound lean beef, cut into small ⅛-inch-thick slices, seasoned*
1 *ounce dry white wine*
¼ *teaspoon cinnamon*
⅛ *teaspoon coriander*
¹⁄₁₆ *teaspoon ground cloves*
¼ *teaspoon fennel seed, ground in a mortar*
1 *tablespoon red currant jelly*
1 *cup pitted cherries, halved*

- Melt margarine in 10-inch pan. Fry beef for 2 minutes over medium to high heat, stirring briskly and turning pieces to cook evenly.
- Add wine and fry 1 minute more, stirring. Remove beef from pan and keep hot.
- Fry spices in same pan for a few seconds, stirring (add margarine if needed). Add jelly and blend in quickly. Add cherries and fry 1 minute more, stirring constantly.
- Return beef to pan and toss quickly. Serve hot.

Chili Beef

3 *tablespoons peanut oil*
1 *garlic clove, minced*
1 *teaspoon chili powder*
½ *teaspoon ground cumin*
1 *pound lean beef, cut into small ⅛-inch-thick slices, seasoned*
1 *medium onion, thinly sliced*

- Heat oil in 12-inch pan. Fry garlic and spices over medium to high heat for a few seconds, stirring.
- Add beef and onion; fry 3 minutes more, stirring briskly and turning beef to let it cook evenly. Serve hot.

Clam-Sauced Beef

1 *tablespoon Italian olive oil*
1 *tablespoon margarine*
1 *garlic clove, minced*
½ *teaspoon parsley*
⅛ *teaspoon oregano*
1 *pound lean beef, cut into small ⅛-inch-thick slices, seasoned*
8 *small clams, shucked, chopped, juices reserved*
1 *scallion, cut into thin strips*
1 *ounce dry white wine*
1 *tablespoon tomato paste*
1 *teaspoon cornstarch blended with 1 tablespoon clam juice*

• Heat oil and margarine in 10-inch pan. Fry garlic and herbs over medium to high heat for a few seconds, stirring.

• Add beef and fry 1 minute more, stirring briskly and turning pieces to cook evenly. Add clams and their juices; fry 1 minute, stirring. Add scallion and fry 1 minute more, stirring.

• Add wine and tomato paste; blend in quickly. Add cornstarch and clam juice slurry; stir in briskly to blend and thicken. Serve hot.

Creole Beef

3 *tablespoons margarine*
1 *garlic clove, minced*
1 *teaspoon chopped chives*
½ *teaspoon parsley*
⅛ *teaspoon cloves*
⅛ *teaspoon ground bay leaf*
1 *ounce Madeira*
1 *pound lean beef, cut into small ⅛-inch-thick slices, seasoned with salt and a dash red pepper (cayenne)*
½ *medium onion, thinly sliced*
1 *medium tomato, halved, sliced, and salted*

• Melt margarine in 12-inch pan. Fry garlic, chives, and spices over medium to high heat for a few seconds, stirring.

• Add Madeira and blend in quickly. Add beef and onion; fry 2 minutes more, stirring briskly and turning beef pieces to cook evenly. Add tomato and fry 2 minutes more, stirring. Serve hot.

Stir-Fried Beef with Egg Garnish

3 tablespoons margarine, divided
2 eggs, seasoned, lightly beaten
½ carrot, shaved with a potato peeler
½ cup finely chopped green pepper
1 pound lean beef, cut into small ⅛-inch-thick slices, peppered
1 cup thinly sliced mushrooms
1 scallion, cut into thin strips
1 cup bean sprouts
1 tablespoon soy sauce

• Melt 1 tablespoon of the margarine in 10-inch pan. Fry eggs over medium heat until they set in a flat omelet. Set aside and keep hot.

• Meanwhile, melt remaining 2 tablespoons margarine in 12-inch pan. Fry carrot shavings and green pepper for 1 minute over medium to high heat, stirring briskly. Add beef and mushrooms to same pan; fry 2 minutes more, stirring briskly and turning pieces to cook evenly. Add scallion, bean sprouts, and soy sauce; fry 1 minute more, stirring.

• Serve beef mixture hot, topped with omelet that is cut in strips.

Farmhouse Beef

4 tablespoons margarine, divided
¾ pound potatoes, peeled and finely diced
1 medium onion, thinly sliced
½ teaspoon parsley
¼ teaspoon tarragon
1 pound lean beef, cut into small ⅛-inch-thick slices, seasoned
¼ pound mushrooms, thinly sliced
⅛ pound lean Canadian bacon, or ham, cut into small thin strips

• Melt half the margarine in a 12-inch pan and the other half in a 10-inch pan.

• Add potatoes and onion to 10-inch pan; stir and cover, cooking over medium to high heat.

• Fry herbs in 12-inch pan over medium to high heat for a few seconds, stirring. Add beef, mushrooms, and bacon to same pan and stir into spicy margarine.

• Continue frying in both pans for 4 minutes more, stirring beef briskly and turning pieces to cook evenly, and stirring potatoes as much as possible. Gently toss the potato and beef mixtures together and serve hot.

Ginger Beef

2 *tablespoons peanut oil*
1 *tablespoon minced crystallized*
  ginger
1 *pound lean beef, cut into small*
  ⅛-inch-thick slices, seasoned
1 *scallion, cut into small strips*

- Heat oil in 10-inch pan. Fry ginger over medium to high heat for a few seconds, stirring.
- Add beef and fry 2 minutes more, stirring briskly and turning pieces to cook evenly. Add scallions and fry 1 minute, stirring. Serve hot.

Beef with Horseradish Sauce

2 *tablespoons margarine*
½ *teaspoon ginger*
⅛ *teaspoon nutmeg*
⅛ *teaspoon ground bay leaf*
¼ *teaspoon marjoram*
½ *onion, thinly sliced*
¼ *cup lean, diced Canadian*
  bacon or ham
1 *pound lean beef, cut into*
  all ⅛-inch-thick slices,
  seasoned
¼ *cup sour cream*
2 *teaspoons prepared*
  horseradish

- Melt margarine in 12-inch pan. Fry spices over medium to high heat for a few seconds, stirring.
- Add onion and fry 30 seconds more, stirring briskly. Add bacon and beef; fry 2½ minutes more, stirring and turning pieces to cook evenly.
- Remove from heat. Add sour cream and blend in quickly. Add horseradish and blend in quickly. Serve hot.

Madeira Beef with Ham

3 *tablespoons margarine*
½ *garlic clove, minced*
2 *teaspoons chopped celery leaves*
1 *teaspoon chopped chives*
⅛ *teaspoon ground bay leaf*
⅛ *teaspoon ground cloves*
⅛ *teaspoon thyme*
½ *small onion, very thinly sliced*
1 *pound lean beef, cut into all ⅛-inch-thick slices, seasoned*
½ *cup thin, lean ham strips*
½ *cup Madeira, hot*
2 *teaspoons cornstarch blended with 1 tablespoon cold Madeira*

• Melt margarine in 12-inch pan. Fry garlic, celery, chives, and spices over medium to high heat for a few seconds, stirring.

• Add onion and fry 30 seconds more, stirring briskly. Add beef and ham; fry 3 minutes more, stirring and turning pieces to cook evenly.

• Add Madeira and boil 10 seconds, stirring. Add cornstarch and Madeira slurry; stir briskly to blend and thicken. Serve hot.

Mediterranean Beef

2 *tablespoons Italian olive oil*
½ *teaspoon parsley*
¼ *teaspoon tarragon*
1 *pound lean beef, cut into small ⅛-inch-thick slices, seasoned*
12 *pitted black olives, thinly sliced*
6 *anchovy strips, drained and minced*

• Heat oil in 10-inch pan. Fry herbs over medium to high heat for a few seconds, stirring.

• Add beef and fry 1 minute more, stirring briskly and turning pieces to cook evenly. Add olives and fry 2 minutes more, stirring. Add anchovies and mix in gently. Serve hot.

Beef and Mushrooms with Madeira Sauce

3 *tablespoons margarine*
½ *teaspoon parsley*
¼ *teaspoon thyme*
⅛ *teaspoon ground bay leaf*
¼ *cup minced onion*
1 *pound lean beef, cut into small ⅛-inch-thick slices, seasoned*
2 *cups thinly sliced mushrooms*
¼ *cup Madeira, hot*
¼ *cup beef stock or broth, preferably unsalted, hot*
2 *teaspoons cornstarch blended with 1 tablespoon cold beef stock*

• Melt margarine in 12-inch pan. Fry spices over medium to high heat for a few seconds, stirring.

• Add onion and fry 30 seconds more, stirring briskly. Add beef and mushrooms; fry 4 minutes, stirring briskly and turning pieces to cook evenly.

• Add wine and stock; fry 30 seconds more, stirring. Add cornstarch and stock slurry; stir in briskly to blend and thicken. Serve hot.

Mustard Beef

2 *tablespoons margarine*
1 *pound lean beef, cut into small ⅛-inch-thick slices, seasoned*
1 *ounce brandy*
¼ *cup dry white wine, hot*
¼ *cup beef stock or broth, preferably unsalted, hot*
2 *teaspoons prepared mild mustard (or hot mustard if you prefer)*
1 *tablespoon cornstarch blended with 2 tablespoons cream*

• Melt margarine in 10-inch pan. Fry beef for 2 minutes over medium to high heat, stirring briskly and turning pieces to cook evenly.

• Flame with brandy, stirring until fire dies. Add wine and stock; fry 1 minute more, stirring.

• Blend in mustard quickly. Add cornstarch and cream slurry; stir in briskly to blend and thicken. Serve hot.

Pan-Barbecued Beef

2 tablespoons Italian olive oil
2 tablespoons minced onion
2 garlic cloves, minced
¼ teaspoon oregano
⅛ teaspoon basil
1 pound lean beef, cut into small ⅛-inch-thick slices, seasoned
¼ cup ketchup
1 tablespoon Worcestershire sauce
2 teaspoons cider vinegar
1 teaspoon lemon juice

- Heat oil in 10-inch pan. Fry onion, garlic, and herbs over medium to high heat for a few seconds, stirring.

- Add beef and fry 2 minutes more, stirring briskly and turning pieces to cook evenly.

- Add ketchup and Worcestershire and blend quickly. Add vinegar and lemon juice and blend quickly. Serve hot.

Quick Beef au Poivre

2 tablespoons margarine
1 teaspoon crushed black peppercorns (or to taste)
1 pound lean beef, cut into small ⅛-inch-thick slices, lightly salted
2 ounces brandy, warm
¼ cup cream or milk, hot
¼ cup beef stock or broth, preferably unsalted, hot
1 tablespoon cornstarch blended with 1 tablespoon cold beef stock

- Melt margarine in 10-inch pan. Fry peppercorns over medium to high heat for a few seconds, stirring constantly.

- Add beef and fry 3 minutes more, stirring briskly and turning pieces to cook evenly. Flame with brandy, stirring until fire dies.

- Add cream and blend in quickly. Add stock and blend in quickly. Add cornstarch and stock slurry; stir in briskly to thicken. Serve hot.

Paprika Beef

3 *tablespoons margarine*
1 *medium onion, very thinly sliced*
1 *garlic clove, minced*
½ *tablespoon paprika*
½ *teaspoon caraway seeds, ground in a mortar*
¼ *teaspoon marjoram*
1 *pound lean beef, cut into small ⅛-inch-thick slices, seasoned*
1 *ounce dry white wine*

- Melt margarine in 12-inch pan. Fry onion for 1 minute over medium to high heat, stirring briskly.

- Remove onion, squeezing out margarine so it remains in pan. Keep onion hot.

- Fry garlic, paprika, and spices in pan for a few seconds, stirring. Add beef and fry 3 minutes more, stirring and turning pieces to cook evenly. Add wine and blend quickly.

- Return onion to pan and stir quickly. Serve hot.

Seedy Beef

2 *tablespoons margarine*
1 *teaspoon caraway seeds, crushed in a mortar*
¼ *teaspoon thyme, ground in a mortar*
1 *pound lean beef, cut into small ⅛-inch-thick slices, seasoned*

- Melt margarine in 10-inch pan. Fry spices over medium to high heat for a few seconds, stirring.

- Add beef and fry 3 minutes more, stirring briskly and turning pieces to cook evenly. Serve hot.

Soy Beef

2 *tablespoons peanut oil*
1 *garlic clove, minced*
2 *tablespoons minced onion*
1 *pound lean beef, cut into small ⅛-inch-thick slices, peppered*
2 *tablespoons soy sauce*

- Heat oil in 10-inch pan. Fry garlic and onion over medium to high heat for a few seconds, stirring.

- Add beef and fry 3 minutes more, stirring briskly and turning pieces to cook evenly. Add soy sauce and blend in quickly. Serve hot.

Spicy Onion Beef

3 tablespoons vegetable oil
½ teaspoon cinnamon
½ teaspoon coriander
½ teaspoon cumin
¼ teaspoon turmeric
⅛ teaspoon nutmeg
⅛ teaspoon ground bay leaf
1/16 teaspoon ground cloves
1 minced onion
1 pound lean beef, cut into
    small ⅛-inch-thick slices,
    seasoned
2 tablespoons plain yogurt
2 tablespoons tomato sauce

- Heat oil in 12-inch pan. Fry spices over medium to high heat for a few seconds, stirring.

- Add onion and fry 30 seconds more, stirring briskly. Add beef; fry 3 minutes more, stirring and turning pieces to cook evenly. Set off heat to cool for a minute.

- Add yogurt and tomato sauce, off heat, and blend in quickly. Serve hot.

Quick Beef Teriyaki

1 pound lean beef, cut into
    small ⅛-inch-thick slices,
½ teaspoon ground ginger
2 tablespoons sake
1 tablespoon soy sauce
1 garlic clove, finely minced
2 tablespoons peanut oil

- Sprinkle beef with ginger and toss together in a shallow bowl for a few seconds.

- Add sake, soy sauce, and garlic; toss together for 30 seconds more.

- Heat oil in 10-inch pan. Fry beef mixture in oil for 3 minutes over medium to high heat, stirring briskly and turning the pieces to cook them evenly. Serve hot.

Liver with Mustard Cream Sauce

3 tablespoons margarine
½ teaspoon dry mustard
1 garlic clove, minced
2 tablespoons minced onion
¾ pound calves' liver, cut into small ¼-inch-thick slices, seasoned and lightly floured
1 ounce dry white wine
½ cup beef stock or broth, preferably unsalted, hot
1 ounce cream
1 tablespoon chopped capers
½ tablespoon cornstarch blended with 1 tablespoon cold stock

• Melt margarine in 12-inch pan. Fry mustard, garlic, and onion for 30 seconds over medium to high heat, stirring.

• Add liver and fry 3 minutes over medium heat, turning pieces to cook evenly.

• Add wine and stock and fry 1 minute more, stirring gently. Add cream and capers; blend in quickly but gently.

• Add cornstarch and stock slurry and stir in quickly but gently to thicken. Serve hot.

Liver and Onions with Apple

3 tablespoons margarine
2 bacon strips, chopped
1 medium onion, thinly sliced
¾ pound calves' liver, cut into small ¼-inch-thick slices, seasoned and lightly floured
1 large apple, peeled, cored, and thinly sliced
½ cup cider or apple juice, hot
2 teaspoons cornstarch blended with 1 tablespoon cold cider

• Melt margarine in 12-inch pan. Fry bacon over medium to high heat for a few seconds, stirring.

• Add onion and fry 30 seconds more, stirring briskly.

• Add liver and fry 2 minutes, turning pieces to cook evenly. Add apple and fry 1 minute, tossing gently.

• Add cider and fry 1 minute, covered. Add cornstarch and cider slurry; stir in quickly but gently to blend and thicken. Serve hot.

Liver with Scallions

3 *tablespoons margarine*
1 *tablespoon sesame seed*
½ *teaspoon ground ginger*
1 *garlic clove, minced*
¾ *pound calves' liver, cut into*
   small ¼-inch-thick slices,
   peppered and lightly
   floured
2 *scallions, cut into thin strips*
1 *tablespoon soy sauce*
1 *ounce Madeira*

- Melt margarine in 12-inch pan. Fry spices and garlic over medium to high heat for a few seconds, stirring.

- Add liver and fry 3 minutes more, turning pieces once during cooking.

- Add scallions and fry 1 minute, tossing gently. Add soy sauce and Madeira; blend in quickly but gently. Serve hot.

Warm Spiced Liver

3 *tablespoons margarine*
1 *tablespoon crystallized*
   ginger, minced
¼ *teaspoon cinnamon*
⅛ *teaspoon nutmeg*
⅛ *teaspoon turmeric*
¹⁄₁₆ *teaspoon ground cloves*
2 *garlic cloves, minced*
1 *medium onion, thinly sliced*
¾ *pound calves' liver, cut into*
   small ¼-inch-thick slices,
   seasoned and lightly floured

- Melt margarine in 12-inch pan. Fry spices and garlic over medium to high heat for a few seconds, stirring.

- Add onion and fry 30 seconds more, stirring briskly.

- Add liver and fry 4 minutes, turning pieces to cook evenly (push onions aside). Serve hot.

PORK

Pork with Apples

2 tablespoons margarine
¼ teaspoon cinnamon
⅛ teaspoon nutmeg
1/16 teaspoon ground cloves
1 pound lean pork, cut into
⅛-inch-thick slices,
seasoned
1 apple, peeled, cored, and
thinly sliced
¼ cup dry white wine, hot
¼ cup cider or apple juice, hot
1 tablespoon honey
1 tablespoon cream (optional)
2 teaspoons cornstarch blended
with 1 tablespoon cold
cider

- Melt margarine in 12-inch pan. Fry spices over medium to high heat for a few seconds, stirring.

- Add pork and fry 2 minutes more, stirring briskly and turning pieces to cook evenly. Add apple and fry 1 minute, stirring gently. Add wine and cider and fry 1 minute more, stirring gently.

- Add honey and cream and blend in quickly but gently. Add cornstarch and cider slurry; stir in quickly but gently to thicken. Serve hot.

Pork with Apricots and Cherries

2 tablespoons margarine
¼ teaspoon ground bay leaf
¼ teaspoon nutmeg
⅛ teaspoon ground cloves
1 pound lean pork, cut into
small ⅛-inch-thick slices,
seasoned
1 ounce kirsch (cherry brandy)
½ cup chicken stock or broth,
preferably unsalted, hot
1 tablespoon maraschino-cherry
juice
1 tablespoon apple jelly
1 tablespoon cornstarch
blended with 1 tablespoon
cold stock
1 cup sliced apricots
½ cup pitted cherries, halved

- Melt margarine in 12-inch pan. Fry spices over medium to high heat for a few seconds, stirring.

- Add pork and fry 3 minutes more, stirring briskly and turning pieces to cook evenly. Flame with kirsch, stirring until fire dies.

- Add stock and cherry juice; fry 1 minute, stirring. Add apple jelly and blend in quickly.

- Add cornstarch and stock slurry; stir in quickly to blend and thicken. Add apricots and cherries and fry a few seconds, stirring gently. Serve hot.

Basque Pork

3 tablespoons Italian olive oil
2 garlic cloves, minced
½ teaspoon parsley
¼ teaspoon basil
¼ teaspoon oregano
½ cup minced onion
¼ cup minced green pepper
1 pound lean pork, cut into
   small ⅛-inch-thick slices,
   seasoned
½ cup lean ham strips
½ cup beef stock or broth,
   preferably unsalted, hot
2 teaspoons cornstarch blended
   with 1 tablespoon cold stock

- Heat oil in 12-inch pan. Fry garlic and herbs over medium to high heat for a few seconds, stirring.

- Add onion and pepper and fry 30 seconds more, stirring briskly.

- Add pork; fry 3 minutes, stirring and turning pieces to cook evenly. Add ham and stock and fry 1 minute more, stirring gently.

- Add cornstarch and stock slurry; stir in quickly but gently to blend and thicken. Serve hot.

Pork with Crab Meat

3 tablespoons peanut oil
½ teaspoon ginger
1 pound lean pork, cut into
   small ⅛-inch-thick slices,
   peppered
¼ cup thinly sliced mushrooms
¼ cup thinly sliced bamboo
   shoots
½ cup crab meat or tiny shrimp,
   cleaned
2 scallions, cut into thin strips
1 tablespoon soy sauce
1 ounce Madeira

- Heat oil in 12-inch pan. Fry ginger over medium to high heat for a few seconds, stirring.

- Add pork and fry 2 minutes more, stirring briskly and turning pieces to cook evenly.

- Add mushrooms and bamboo shoots; fry 1 minute, stirring. Add crab meat and scallions and fry 2 minutes more, stirring. Add soy sauce and Madeira; blend in quickly. Serve hot.

Cucumber Pork

2 *tablespoons margarine*
1 *pound lean pork, cut into small ⅛-inch-thick slices, seasoned*
1 *cucumber, peeled, halved lengthwise, thinly sliced, salted*
1 *ounce dry white wine, hot*
¼ *cup chicken stock or broth, preferably unsalted, hot*
2 *teaspoons cornstarch blended with 1 tablespoon cold stock*

- Melt margarine in 12-inch pan. Fry pork for 3 minutes over medium to high heat, stirring briskly and turning pieces to cook evenly.

- Add cucumber and fry 1 minute more, stirring. Add wine and stock; fry 1 minute more, stirring.

- Add cornstarch and stock slurry; stir in briskly to blend and thicken. Serve hot.

Egg Soy Pork

1 *tablespoon margarine*
2 *eggs, beaten with 1 tablespoon soy sauce and pepper to taste*
2 *tablespoons peanut oil*
2 *garlic cloves, minced*
1 *pound lean pork, cut into small ⅛-inch-thick slices, peppered*
1 *cup bean sprouts*
2 *scallions, cut into thin strips*
1 *tablespoon soy sauce*
1 *ounce dry white wine*

- Melt margarine in a 10-inch pan. Fry eggs over medium to high heat, making a flat omelet. When done, set aside and keep hot.

- Meanwhile, heat oil in a 12-inch pan. Fry garlic over medium to high heat for a few seconds, stirring. Add pork and fry 2 minutes more, stirring briskly and turning pieces to cook evenly.

- Add bean sprouts and scallions; fry 1 minute, stirring. Add soy sauce and wine, and fry another minute more, stirring. Serve hot, topped with the omelet cut in strips.

Fennel Pork

2 *tablespoons margarine*
1 *garlic clove, minced*
1 *tablespoon fennel seed,*
   crushed in a mortar
1 *pound lean pork, cut into*
   small ⅛-inch-thick slices,
   seasoned
1 *teaspoon lemon juice*
1 *tablespoon orange juice*
¼ *cup cream, hot*

- Melt margarine in 10-inch pan. Fry garlic and fennel seed over medium to high heat for a few seconds, stirring.

- Add pork and fry 3 minutes more, stirring briskly and turning pieces to cook evenly.

- Sprinkle with lemon and orange juices; fry 1 minute more, stirring. Add cream and boil about 1 minute over very high heat, stirring until volume is reduced by half. Serve hot.

Flemish Pork

3 *tablespoons margarine*
1 *onion, thinly sliced*
1 *pound pork, cut into small*
   ⅛-inch-thick slices,
   seasoned
1 *ounce gin*
4 *juniper berries, finely crushed*
   in a mortar
¼ *cup beer, hot*
¼ *cup beef stock or broth,*
   preferably unsalted, hot
2 *teaspoons cornstarch blended*
   with 1 tablespoon cold stock

- Melt margarine in 12-inch pan. Fry onion for 1 minute over medium to high heat, stirring briskly.

- Add pork and fry 2 minutes more, stirring and turning pieces to cook evenly. Flame with gin, stirring until fire dies.

- Add juniper berries, beer, and stock; fry 1 minute more, stirring. Add cornstarch and stock slurry and stir in briskly to blend and thicken. Serve hot.

Pork and Mushrooms with Tomato Sauce

3 tablespoons margarine,
    divided
½ teaspoon parsley
¼ teaspoon oregano
¼ teaspoon basil
2 garlic cloves, minced
¼ cup minced onion
2 cups chopped and mashed
    tomato, juices reserved,
    seasoned
1 pound lean pork, cut into
    small ⅛-inch-thick slices,
    seasoned
½ cup thinly sliced mushrooms

- Melt 1 tablespoon of the margarine in a 10-inch pan. Fry herbs, garlic, and onion over medium to high heat for a few seconds, stirring.

- Add tomato and juices; fry 30 seconds more, stirring briskly.

- Melt remaining 2 tablespoons margarine in a 12-inch pan. Fry pork for 1 minute over high heat, stirring briskly and turning pieces to cook evenly. Continue frying tomatoes, stirring occasionally.

- Add mushrooms to pork and fry 3 minutes more, stirring. Continue frying tomatoes, stirring occasionally. Serve pork and mushrooms hot and spoon tomato sauce over top.

Mustard Sesame Pork

2 tablespoons peanut oil
2 tablespoons sesame seed,
    crushed in a mortar
1 pound lean pork, cut into
    small ⅛-inch-thick slices,
    peppered
1 small onion, thinly sliced
1 tablespoon soy sauce
1 ounce sake
1 tablespoon prepared mustard

- Heat oil in 10-inch pan. Fry sesame seeds over medium to high heat for a few seconds, stirring.

- Add pork and fry 2 minutes more, stirring briskly and turning pieces to cook evenly. Add onion and fry 2 minutes, stirring.

- Add soy sauce and blend in quickly. Add sake and stir in quickly. Add mustard and blend in quickly. Serve hot.

Pork with Olives

2 *tablespoons margarine*
1 *pound lean pork, cut into small ⅛-inch-thick slices, seasoned*
¼ *cup thinly sliced, pitted green olives*
¼ *cup thinly sliced, pitted black olives*
½ *cup beer, hot*
2 *teaspoons cornstarch blended with 1 tablespoon cold beer*

• Melt margarine in 12-inch pan. Fry pork for 3 minutes over medium to high heat, stirring briskly and turning pieces to cook evenly.

• Add olives and fry 1 minute more, stirring gently. Add beer and fry 30 seconds more, stirring gently.

• Add cornstarch and beer slurry; stir in quickly but gently to blend and thicken. Serve hot.

Onion Pork

3 *tablespoons peanut oil*
1 *pound lean pork, cut into small ⅛-inch-thick slices, peppered*
2 *cups thinly sliced onions*
1 *tablespoon soy sauce*
½ *teaspoon sugar*
1 *ounce dry white wine*
½ *cup chicken stock or broth, preferably unsalted, hot*
2 *teaspoons cornstarch blended with 1 tablespoon cold stock*

• Heat oil in 12-inch pan. Fry pork for 1 minute over medium to high heat, stirring briskly and turning pieces to cook evenly.

• Add onions and fry 2 minutes more, stirring. Add soy sauce and blend in quickly. Add sugar and blend in quickly.

• Add wine and stock and fry 1 minute more, stirring. Add cornstarch and stock slurry; stir in briskly to blend and thicken. Serve hot.

Pork with Orange Sauce

2 tablespoons margarine
2 teaspoons grated orange rind
½ teaspoon ground ginger
1 garlic clove, minced
¼ cup minced onion
1 pound lean pork, cut into
small ⅛-inch-thick slices,
seasoned
1 ounce curaçao liqueur
(orange liqueur)
½ cup chicken stock or broth,
preferably unsalted, hot
1 tablespoon cornstarch
blended with 1 tablespoon
dry white wine

• Melt margarine in 10-inch pan. Fry orange rind, ginger, garlic, and onion over medium to high heat for a few seconds, stirring.

• Add pork and fry 2 minutes more, stirring briskly and turning pieces to cook evenly. Flame with curaçao, stirring until fire dies.

• Add stock and fry 1 minute more, stirring. Add cornstarch and wine slurry; stir in briskly to blend and thicken. Serve hot.

Paprika Pork

2 tablespoons margarine
1 garlic clove, minced
½ teaspoon parsley
¼ teaspoon rosemary
1 pound lean pork, cut into
small ⅛-inch-thick slices,
seasoned
½ teaspoon paprika
2 cups chopped and mashed
tomato, juices reserved,
lightly salted
1 teaspoon minced chili pepper
1 tablespoon tomato paste
blended with 1 ounce dry
white wine

• Melt margarine in 12-inch pan. Fry garlic and herbs over medium to high heat for a few seconds, stirring.

• Add pork and brown for 1 minute, stirring briskly and turning pieces to brown evenly. Add paprika and blend in quickly.

• Add tomato and juices and fry 3 minutes, stirring. Add chili pepper and tomato mixture; fry 30 seconds more, stirring. Serve hot.

Pork with Peanuts and Chives

2 tablespoons margarine
½ teaspoon parsley
¼ teaspoon tarragon
⅛ teaspoon ground bay leaf
1 pound lean pork, cut into
 small ⅛-inch-thick slices,
 seasoned
½ cup peanuts
¼ cup chopped chives

- Melt margarine in 12-inch pan. Fry herbs over medium to high heat for a few seconds, stirring.
- Add pork, peanuts, and chives; fry 4 minutes more, stirring briskly and turning pieces to cook evenly. Serve hot.

Curried Pork with Pears

3 tablespoons margarine
½ teaspoon cinnamon
¼ teaspoon coriander
¼ teaspoon turmeric
⅛ teaspoon nutmeg
⅛ teaspoon fenugreek
⅛ teaspoon ground bay leaf
¹⁄₁₆ teaspoon ground cloves
1 pound lean pork, cut into
 small ⅛-inch-thick slices,
 seasoned with salt and a
 dash red pepper (cayenne)
1½ cups thin pear slices
¼ cup dry white wine, hot
¼ cup beef stock or broth,
 preferably unsalted, hot
2 teaspoons lemon juice
1 tablespoon honey
2 teaspoons cornstarch
 blended with 1 tablespoon
 cold dry white wine

- Melt margarine in 12-inch pan. Fry spices over medium to high heat for a few seconds, stirring.
- Add pork and fry 3 minutes more, stirring briskly and turning pieces to cook evenly.
- Add pears and fry 30 seconds, stirring gently. Add wine and stock; fry 30 seconds more, stirring gently.
- Add lemon juice and honey and blend in quickly but gently. Add cornstarch and wine slurry; stir in quickly but gently to thicken. Serve hot.

Pork with Port Sauce

3 tablespoons margarine
½ teaspoon parsley
⅛ teaspoon thyme
⅛ teaspoon ground bay leaf
½ carrot, shaved with a potato peeler
½ celery stalk, finely minced
½ small onion, minced
1 pound lean pork, cut into small ⅛-inch-thick slices, seasoned
¼ cup port wine, hot
¼ cup beef stock or broth, preferably unsalted, hot
2 teaspoons cornstarch blended with 1 tablespoon cold stock

• Melt margarine in 12-inch pan. Fry herbs over medium to high heat for a few seconds, stirring.

• Add carrot shavings, celery, and onion; fry 30 seconds more, stirring briskly.

• Add pork and fry 3 minutes, stirring and turning pieces to cook evenly. Add port and stock and fry 30 seconds more, stirring.

• Add cornstarch and stock slurry; stir in briskly to blend and thicken. Serve hot.

Pork with Snow Peas

3 tablepoons peanut oil
¼ teaspoon ginger
½ teaspoon sesame seeds, crushed in a mortar
1 pound lean pork, cut into small ⅛-inch-thick slices, peppered
1½ cups snow peas
2 teaspoons soy sauce
1 tablespoon Madeira

• Heat oil in 12-inch pan. Fry ginger and sesame seeds over medium to high heat for a few seconds, stirring.

• Add pork and fry 2 minutes more, stirring briskly and turning pieces to cook evenly.

• Add snow peas and fry 1 minute, stirring. Add soy sauce and Madeira wine; fry 1 minute more, stirring in briskly to blend. Serve hot.

Spice-Barbecued Pork

2 *tablespoons peanut oil*
1 *garlic clove, minced*
¼ *teaspoon cinnamon*
⅛ *teaspoon nutmeg*
¹⁄₁₆ *teaspoon ground cloves*
¼ *teaspoon anise seed, crushed in a mortar*
1 *pound lean pork, cut into small ⅛-inch-thick slices, peppered*
1 *ounce brandy*
1 *tablespoon soy sauce*

• Heat oil in 10-inch pan. Fry garlic and spices over medium to high heat for a few seconds, stirring.

• Add pork and fry 3 minutes more, stirring briskly and turning pieces to cook evenly. Flame with brandy, stirring until fire dies.

• Add soy sauce and fry 1 minute more, stirring. Serve hot.

Spiced Pork

3 *tablespoons margarine*
1 *garlic clove, minced*
1 *tablespoon crystallized ginger, minced*
⅛ *teaspoon cinnamon*
⅛ *teaspoon mace*
⅛ *teaspoon ground cloves*
⅛ *teaspoon ground bay leaf*
½ *medium onion, thinly sliced*
½ *celery stalk, very thinly sliced*
1 *pound lean pork, cut into small ⅛-inch-thick slices*
1½ *tablespoons soy sauce*
1 *teaspoon chili pepper, finely minced*

• Melt margarine in 12-inch pan. Fry garlic, ginger, and spices over medium to high heat for a few seconds, stirring.

• Add onion and celery; fry 30 seconds more, stirring briskly.

• Add pork and fry 3 minutes, stirring and turning pieces to cook evenly.

• Add soy sauce and chili pepper and fry 1 minute more, stirring. Serve hot.

Strawberry Pork

2 tablespoons margarine
1 pound lean pork, cut into
    small 1/8-inch-thick slices,
    seasoned
1 ounce Grand Marnier or
    brandy of your choice
½ cup cider or apple juice, hot
2 teaspoons red currant jelly
1½ cups sliced strawberries
1 tablespoon cornstarch
    blended with 1 tablespoon
    cold cider

• Melt margarine in 12-inch pan. Fry pork for 2 minutes over medium to high heat, stirring briskly and turning pieces to cook evenly. Flame with Grand Marnier, stirring until fire dies.

• Add cider and fry 1 minute, stirring. Add jelly and blend in quickly. Add strawberries and fry 30 seconds more, tossing very gently.

• Add cornstarch and cider slurry; stir in quickly but very gently to blend and thicken. Serve hot.

Tomato Mustard Pork

2 tablespoons margarine
1 garlic clove, minced
2 tablespoons minced onion
½ teaspoon parsley
¼ teaspoon oregano
1 pound lean pork, cut into
    small 1/8-inch-thick slices,
    seasoned
1 tablespoon capers
1 tablespoon prepared mustard
¼ cup tomato sauce
1 tablespoon chopped chives

• Melt margarine in 10-inch pan. Fry garlic, onion, and herbs over medium to high heat for a few seconds, stirring.

• Add pork and fry 3 minutes more, stirring briskly and turning pieces to cook evenly.

• Add capers and fry 1 minute, stirring. Add mustard, tomato sauce, and chives, stirring to blend in well. Serve hot.

Spicy Tomato-Sauced Pork

2 tablespoons margarine
2 garlic cloves, minced
½ teaspoon chili powder
¼ teaspoon ginger
¼ teaspoon cumin
⅛ teaspoon turmeric
⅛ teaspoon coriander
1/16 teaspoon mace
1/16 teaspoon ground cloves
1 pound lean pork, cut into
   small ⅛-inch-thick slices,
   seasoned
1 ounce brandy
½ cup tomato sauce, hot

• Melt margarine in 10-inch pan. Fry garlic and spices over medium to high heat for a few seconds, stirring.

• Add pork and fry 3 minutes more, stirring briskly and turning pieces to cook evenly. Flame with brandy, stirring until fire dies.

• Add tomato sauce and fry 1 minute more, stirring. Serve hot.

Pork with Water Chestnuts

2 tablespoons peanut oil
½ teaspoon ginger
1 cup chopped water chestnuts
1 pound lean pork, cut into
   small ⅛-inch-thick slices,
   peppered
3 scallions, cut into thin strips
1 tablespoon soy sauce
1 ounce Madeira

• Heat oil in 12-inch pan. Fry ginger over medium to high heat for a few seconds, stirring. Add water chestnuts and fry 30 seconds more, stirring briskly.

• Add pork and fry 2 minutes, stirring. Add scallions and fry 1 minute more, stirring.

• Add soy sauce and Madeira; fry 1 minute more, stirring. Serve hot.

Pork with Watercress

2 tablespoons Italian olive oil
1 garlic clove, minced
½ teaspoon rosemary
¼ teaspoon thyme
½ teaspoon sage
¼ teaspoon ground bay leaf
1 pound lean pork, cut into
    small ⅛-inch-thick slices,
    seasoned
2 tablespoons watercress leaves

• Heat oil in 10-inch pan. Fry garlic and herbs over medium to high heat for a few seconds, stirring.

• Add pork and fry 4 minutes more, stirring briskly and turning pieces to cook evenly. Serve hot, garnished with watercress.

Ham with Beer

2 tablespoons margarine
½ teaspoon parsley
¼ teaspoon oregano
1 pound cooked lean ham, cut
    into small slices, chunks, or
    strips
½ cup beer, hot
1 tablespoon cider vinegar
1 tablespoon molasses
2 teaspoons cornstarch blended
    with 1 tablespoon cold beer

• Melt margarine in 10-inch pan. Fry herbs over medium to high heat for a few seconds, stirring.

• Add ham and fry 1 minute more, stirring briskly and turning pieces to cook evenly.

• Add beer and fry 1 minute, stirring. Add vinegar and molasses and blend in quickly.

• Add cornstarch and beer slurry; stir in briskly to blend and thicken. Serve hot.

Ham with Madeira Sauce

2 *tablespoons margarine*
1 *pound cooked lean ham, cut into slices or chunks*
¼ *cup Madeira*
¼ *cup tomato sauce*

- Melt margarine in 10-inch pan. Fry ham for 1 minute over medium to high heat, stirring briskly and turning pieces to cook evenly.

- Add Madeira and fry 1 minute more, stirring. Add tomato sauce and fry 1 minute or until the sauce thickens, stirring. Serve hot.

Ham with Spinach and Croutons

4 *tablespoons margarine, divided*
1 *package frozen spinach, thawed, drained, seasoned*
1 *cup bread cubes, preferably stale*
1 *pound cooked lean ham, cut into small ⅛-inch-thick slices*

- Melt half the margarine in a 12-inch pan. Add spinach and fry over medium to high heat for 1 minute, stirring.

- Melt remaining half of margarine in a 10-inch pan. Add bread cubes and fry over medium to high heat for 1 minute, stirring.

- Add ham to spinach and fry 2 minutes more, stirring. Continue frying bread cubes stirring until they are golden; then drain on paper towels. Serve ham and spinach hot, topped with croutons.

Ham with Orange-Pineapple Sauce

2 tablespoons margarine
¼ teaspoon cinnamon
⅛ teaspoon nutmeg
⅛ teaspoon ground cloves
1/16 teaspoon cumin
1 pound cooked lean ham, cut into small slices, chunks, or strips
1 ounce Grand Marnier
½ cup chicken stock or broth, preferably unsalted, hot
1 tablespoon orange marmalade
1 tablespoon cornstarch blended with 1 tablespoon cold stock
1 cup pineapple chunks, thinly sliced
½ cup orange sections, halved crosswise, seeds and membranes removed

- Melt margarine in 12-inch pan. Fry spices over medium to high heat for a few seconds, stirring.

- Add ham and fry 1 minute more, stirring. Flame with Grand Marnier, stirring until fire dies.

- Add stock and fry 30 seconds, stirring. Add marmalade and blend in quickly.

- Add cornstarch and stock slurry; stir in quickly to blend and thicken. Add pineapple and orange sections and fry 30 seconds more, tossing gently. Serve hot.

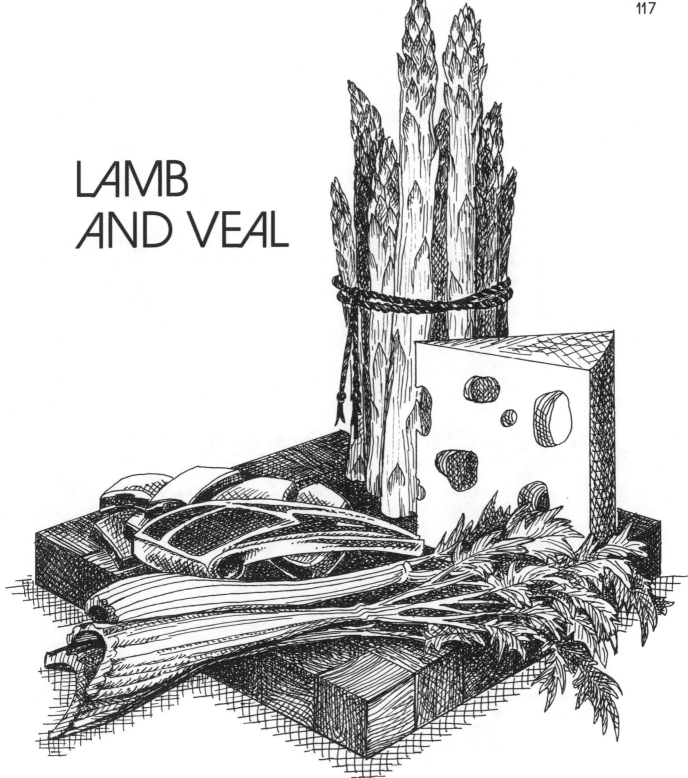

LAMB AND VEAL

Lamb with Almonds and Cashews

2 *tablespoons peanut oil*
½ *teaspoon coriander*
¼ *teaspoon cumin*
⅛ *teaspoon turmeric*
⅛ *teaspoon cinnamon*
⅛ *teaspoon nutmeg*
⅟₁₆ *teaspoon ground cloves*
1 *garlic clove, minced*
1 *pound lean lamb, cut into small ⅛-inch-thick slices, seasoned*
¼ *cup slivered almonds*
¼ *cup cashew nuts*
2 *tablespoons sour cream*
¼ *cup tomato sauce*

- Heat oil in 12-inch pan. Fry spices and garlic over medium to high heat for a few seconds, stirring.

- Add lamb and fry 1 minute more, stirring briskly and turning pieces to cook evenly.

- Add almonds and cashews; fry 2 minutes, stirring. Add sour cream and tomato sauce and blend in quickly. Serve hot.

Lamb with Chinese Vegetables

3 *tablespoons margarine*
2 *tablespoons chopped leek white or onion*
1 *pound lean lamb, cut into small ⅛-inch-thick slices, peppered*
½ *cup thinly sliced bamboo shoots*
½ *cup snow peas*
½ *cup thinly sliced mushrooms*
½ *cup thinly sliced water chestnuts*
2 *tablespoons soy sauce*
½ *cup beef stock or broth, preferably unsalted, hot*
2 *teaspoons cornstarch blended with 1 ounce port*

- Melt margarine in 12-inch pan. Fry leeks over medium to high heat for a few seconds, stirring.

- Add lamb and fry 1 minute more, stirring briskly and turning pieces to cook evenly. Add bamboo shoots and fry 30 seconds, stirring. Add snow peas and fry 30 seconds more, stirring.

- Add mushrooms and water chestnuts; fry 30 seconds, stirring. Blend in soy sauce quickly.

- Add stock and fry 1 minute more, stirring. Add cornstarch and port slurry and stir in quickly but gently to blend and thicken. Serve hot.

Cream-Sauced Lamb

3 *tablespoons margarine*
¼ *teaspoon thyme*
¼ *teaspoon ground bay leaf*
½ *carrot, shaved with a potato peeler*
½ *celery stalk, very thinly sliced*
½ *onion, finely minced*
1 *pound lean lamb, cut into small ⅛-inch-thick slices, seasoned*
  lemon juice to taste
1 *ounce dry white wine*
½ *cup chicken stock or broth, preferably unsalted, hot*
1 *tablespoon cornstarch blended with 2 tablespoons cream*

• Melt margarine in 12-inch pan. Fry herbs, carrot shavings, celery, and onion for 1 minute over medium to high heat, stirring.

• Add lamb and fry 2 minutes more, stirring briskly and turning pieces to cook evenly. Sprinkle with lemon juice to taste.

• Add wine and blend in quickly. Add stock and fry 1 minute more, stirring. Add cornstarch and cream slurry and stir in briskly to blend and thicken. Serve hot.

Lamb with Cucumber and Tomatoes

3 *tablespoons Italian olive oil*
2 *garlic cloves, minced*
½ *teaspoon parsley*
¼ *teaspoon basil*
⅛ *teaspoon oregano*
½ *teaspoon cumin*
¼ *teaspoon turmeric*
½ *medium onion, thinly sliced*
1 *pound lean lamb, cut into small ⅛-inch-thick slices, seasoned*
1 *cup thin cucumber slices, seasoned*
1 *cup chopped tomatoes, salted*

• Heat oil in 12-inch pan. Fry garlic and herbs over medium to high heat for a few seconds, stirring. Add onion and fry 30 seconds more, stirring.

• Add lamb and fry 2 minutes, stirring briskly and turning pieces to cook evenly.

• Add cucumbers and tomatoes; fry 2 minutes more, stirring gently. Serve hot.

Date Onion Lamb

3 *tablespoons margarine*
¼ *teaspoon ginger*
⅛ *teaspoon cinnamon*
⅛ *teaspoon nutmeg*
1/16 *teaspoon ground cloves*
1 *medium onion, thinly sliced*
1 *pound lean lamb, cut into*
   small ⅛-inch-thick slices,
   seasoned
½ *cup sliced dates*
2 *tablespoons plain yogurt*
2 *tablespoons tomato sauce*

- Melt margarine in 12-inch pan. Fry spices and onion for 30 seconds over medium to high heat, stirring.

- Add lamb and fry 3 minutes more, stirring briskly and turning pieces to cook evenly.

- Add dates and fry a few seconds, stirring gently. Add yogurt and tomato sauce and blend in quickly but gently. Serve hot.

Red Egg Lamb

1 *tablespoon margarine*
2 *eggs, seasoned, beaten with*
   2 teaspoons tomato paste
   (First mash tomato paste
   with a little of the egg, then
   add remaining egg, salt, and
   pepper; finish beating.)
2 *tablespoons Italian olive oil*
1 *onion, thinly sliced*
1 *garlic clove, minced*
½ *teaspoon basil*
¼ *teaspoon oregano*
1 *pound lean lamb, cut into*
   small ⅛-inch-thick slices,
   seasoned
½ *cup beef stock or broth,*
   preferably unsalted
   (optional)
2 *teaspoons cornstarch blended*
   with 1 tablespoon stock
   (optional)

- Melt margarine in a 10-inch pan. Fry eggs over medium to high heat, making a flat omelet. When done, set aside and keep hot.

- Meanwhile, heat oil in a 12-inch pan. Fry onion, garlic, and herbs over medium to high heat for a few seconds, stirring.

- Add lamb to onion mixture and fry 3 minutes more, stirring and turning pieces to cook evenly. Remove the lamb mixture to a hot platter and keep hot.

- Add stock to the 12-inch pan and heat through, scraping up the juices. Add cornstarch and stock slurry to the sauce and blend in quickly to thicken. Serve the lamb hot, topped with the omelet cut into strips. Spoon on pan sauce.

Fennel Lamb

2 tablespoons margarine
1 teaspoon fennel seeds, crushed
    in a mortar
1 pound lean lamb, cut into
    small 1/8-inch-thick slices,
    seasoned
1 ounce Chartreuse or Pernod
1/2 cup milk, hot
1 tablespoon cornstarch
    blended with 1 tablespoon
    cold milk

- Melt margarine in 10-inch pan. Fry fennel seeds over medium to high heat for a few seconds, stirring constantly.

- Add lamb and fry 2 minutes more, stirring briskly and turning pieces to cook evenly. Flame with Chartreuse, stirring until fire dies.

- Add milk and fry 1 minute, stirring. Add cornstarch and milk slurry and stir in briskly to blend and thicken. Serve hot.

Lamb with Mint Sauce

2 tablespoons margarine
1 tablespoon chopped fresh
    mint, or 1 teaspoon dried
1 garlic clove, minced
1 pound lean lamb, cut into
    1/8-inch-thick-slices,
    seasoned
    lemon juice to taste
1/2 cup cider or apple juice, hot
1 tablespoon mint jelly
2 teaspoons cornstarch blended
    with 1 tablespoon cold cider

- Melt margarine in 10-inch pan. Fry mint and garlic over medium to high heat for a few seconds, stirring.

- Add lamb and fry 2 minutes more, stirring briskly and turning pieces to cook evenly. Sprinkle with lemon juice to taste (just a few drops).

- Add cider and fry 1 minute more, stirring. Add mint jelly and blend in quickly. Add cornstarch and cider slurry and stir in briskly to blend and thicken. Serve hot.

Lamb with Mustard Cream Sauce

2 tablespoons margarine
½ teaspoon marjoram
¼ teaspoon oregano
⅛ teaspoon rosemary
2 tablespoons minced celery
2 tablespoons minced onion
1 garlic clove, minced
1 pound lean lamb, cut into small ⅛-inch-thick slices, seasoned
1 teaspoon paprika
2 teaspoons prepared mustard
2 tablespoons cream

- Melt margarine in 10-inch pan. Fry herbs, celery, onion, and garlic for 30 seconds over medium to high heat, stirring.

- Add lamb and fry 3 minutes more, stirring briskly and turning pieces to cook evenly.

- Add paprika and mustard; fry a few seconds more, stirring. Add cream and blend in quickly. Serve hot.

Golden Onion Lamb

3 tablespoons margarine
½ teaspoon ginger
¼ teaspoon turmeric
¼ teaspoon cumin
1 onion, thinly sliced
1 pound lean lamb, cut into small ⅛-inch-thick slices, seasoned
1 ounce dry white wine
3 ounces chicken stock or broth, preferably unsalted, hot
2 teaspoons cornstarch blended with 1 tablespoon cold stock

- Melt margarine in 12-inch pan. Fry spices and onion for 30 seconds over medium to high heat, stirring briskly.

- Add lamb and fry 2 minutes more, stirring and turning pieces to cook evenly.

- Add wine and stock; fry 1 minute more, stirring. Add cornstarch and stock slurry and stir in briskly to blend and thicken. Serve hot.

Quick Oriental Lamb

2 tablespoons peanut oil
1 garlic clove, minced
2 teaspoons crystallized ginger, chopped
1 pound lean lamb, cut into small ⅛-inch-thick slices, peppered
3 scallions, cut into thin strips
1 tablespoon soy sauce
1 ounce sherry

- Heat oil in 10-inch pan. Fry garlic and ginger over medium to high heat for a few seconds, stirring.

- Add lamb and fry 2 minutes more, stirring briskly and turning pieces to cook evenly.

- Add scallions and fry 1 minute, stirring. Add soy sauce and sherry and blend in quickly. Serve hot.

Lamb with Peppers

3 tablespoons Italian olive oil
2 garlic cloves, minced
½ teaspoon basil
¼ teaspoon oregano
1 green pepper, seeded and minced
1 red pepper, seeded and minced
1 pound lean lamb, cut into small ⅛-inch-thick slices, seasoned
1 teaspoon minced chili pepper
1 tablespoon capers

- Heat oil in 12-inch pan. Fry garlic and herbs over medium to high heat for a few seconds, stirring. Add green and red peppers and fry 1 minute more, stirring briskly.

- Add lamb and fry 3 minutes, stirring and turning pieces to cook evenly.

- Add chili pepper and blend in quickly. Add capers and blend in quickly. Serve hot.

Rosemary Lamb

1 *tablespoon margarine*
1 *tablespoon Italian olive oil*
½ *teaspoon rosemary*
1 *pound lean lamb, cut into small ⅛-inch-thick slices, seasoned*

- Heat margarine and oil in 10-inch pan. Fry rosemary over medium to high heat for a few seconds, stirring.

- Add the lamb and fry for another 3 minutes, stirring briskly and turning the pieces to cook evenly. Serve hot.

Lamb with Scallions

3 *tablespoons margarine*
½ *teaspoon sesame seeds, crushed in a mortar*
¼ *teaspoon anise seeds, crushed in a mortar*
1 *garlic clove, minced*
1 *pound lean lamb, cut into small ⅛-inch-thick slices, peppered*
6 *scallions, cut into thin strips*
1 *tablespoon soy sauce*
1 *ounce Madeira*
2 *teaspoons cider vinegar*
½ *cup chicken stock or broth, preferably unsalted, hot*
1 *tablespoon cornstarch blended with 1 tablespoon Madeira*

- Melt margarine in 12-inch pan. Fry seeds and garlic over medium to high heat for a few seconds, stirring.

- Add lamb and scallions; fry 2 minutes more, stirring briskly and turning pieces to cook evenly.

- Add soy sauce, Madeira, and vinegar and blend in quickly. Add stock and fry 1 minute, stirring. Add cornstarch and Madeira slurry and stir in briskly to blend and thicken. Serve hot.

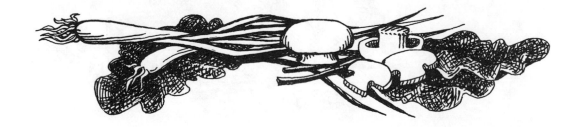

Lamb with Spinach

3 *tablespoons margarine*
2 *teaspoons sesame seeds, crushed in a mortar*
1 *small onion, thinly sliced*
¼ *cup diced lean Canadian bacon or ham*
1 *pound lean lamb, cut into small ⅛-inch-thick slices, seasoned*
½ *cup sliced mushrooms*
1 *package (10 ounces) frozen spinach, thawed and well-drained*
  pepper to taste
1 *tablespoon soy sauce*

- Melt margarine in 12-inch pan. Fry sesame seeds, onion, and bacon over medium to high heat for a few seconds, stirring.

- Add lamb and mushrooms; fry 1 minute more, stirring briskly and turning pieces to cook evenly.

- Add spinach and fry 3 minutes, stirring. Season with pepper. Add soy sauce and blend in quickly. Serve hot.

Tangerine Lamb

2 *tablespoons margarine*
¼ *teaspoon cinnamon*
⅛ *teaspoon nutmeg*
1/16 *teaspoon ground cloves*
1 *pound lean lamb, cut into small ⅛-inch-thick slices, seasoned*
1 *ounce Grand Marnier*
1 *cup tangerine sections, halved crosswise and seeded, membranes removed if desired*
1 *ounce dry white wine*
3 *ounces tangerine juice or orange juice, hot*
1 *tablespoon cornstarch blended with 1 tablespoon Grand Marnier*

- Melt margarine in 12-inch pan. Fry spices over medium to high heat for a few seconds, stirring.

- Add lamb and fry 2 minutes more, stirring briskly and turning pieces to cook evenly. Flame with Grand Marnier, stirring until fire dies.

- Add tangerines and toss quickly but gently. Add wine and tangerine juice; fry 30 seconds more, tossing gently. Add cornstarch and Grand Marnier slurry; stir in quickly but gently to blend and thicken. Serve hot.

Apple Veal

3 tablespoons margarine
¼ teaspoon cinnamon
⅛ teaspoon nutmeg
1/16 teaspoon ground cloves
1 pound veal, cut into small
    ⅛-inch-thick slices,
    seasoned
1 ounce Calvados or brandy of
    your choice
1 apple, peeled, cored, and
    thinly sliced
½ cup cider or apple juice, hot
1 tablespoon red currant jelly
2 teaspoons cornstarch blended
    with 1 tablespoon cold
    cider

• Melt margarine in 12-inch pan. Fry spices over medium to high heat for a few seconds, stirring.

• Add veal and fry 2 minutes more, stirring briskly and turning pieces to cook evenly. Flame with Calvados, stirring until fire dies.

• Add apple and fry 1 minute, stirring gently. Add cider and fry 1 minute more, stirring gently. Blend in jelly quickly but gently. Add cornstarch and cider slurry and stir in quickly but gently to blend and thicken. Serve hot.

Veal with Asparagus

3 tablespoons margarine
1 pound veal, cut into small
    ⅛-inch-thick slices,
    seasoned
1 package (10 ounces) frozen
    asparagus, thawed, cut into
    bite-size pieces, and
    seasoned
1 tablespoon lemon juice (or to
    taste)
¼ cup lean ham strips
2 tablespoons grated Parmesan
    cheese

• Melt margarine in 12-inch pan. Fry veal over medium to high heat, stirring briskly and turning pieces to cook evenly.

• Add asparagus and fry 1 minute more, tossing gently. Add lemon juice and fry 30 seconds, tossing gently.

• Add ham and fry 1 minute more, tossing gently. Add cheese and toss gently to mix and begin melting. Serve hot.

Veal with Basil

2 tablespoons margarine
1 garlic clove, minced
1 teaspoon basil
1 pound veal, cut into small
  1/8-inch-thick slices,
  seasoned
2 scallions, cut into thin strips
1 ounce dry white wine
3 ounces beef stock or broth,
  preferably unsalted, hot
  lemon juice to taste
2 teaspoons cornstarch blended
  with 1 tablespoon dry white
  wine

- Melt margarine in 10-inch pan. Fry garlic and basil over medium to high heat for a few seconds, stirring.

- Add veal and fry 2 minutes more, stirring briskly and turning pieces to cook evenly. Add scallions and fry 1 minute, stirring. Add wine and stock; fry 30 seconds more, stirring.

- Season with lemon juice to taste. Add cornstarch and wine slurry and stir in briskly to blend and thicken. Serve hot.

Veal with Bean Sprouts

3 tablespoons margarine
1 garlic clove, minced
1/2 teaspoon ground ginger
1 pound veal, cut into small
  1/8-inch-thick slices,
  peppered
2 scallions, cut into thin strips
1½ cups bean sprouts
2 tablespoons soy sauce
¼ cup Madeira
2 teaspoons cornstarch
  blended with 1 tablespoon
  Madeira

- Melt margarine in 12-inch pan. Fry garlic and ginger over medium to high heat for a few seconds, stirring.

- Add veal and fry 2 minutes more, stirring briskly and turning pieces to cook evenly. Add scallions and fry 30 seconds, stirring. Add bean sprouts and fry 1 minute more, stirring.

- Add soy sauce and Madeira; fry a few seconds, stirring. Add cornstarch and Madeira slurry and stir in briskly to blend and thicken. Serve hot.

Foie Gras Stuffed Veal

3 *tablespoons margarine*
4 *medium-size veal cutlets,*
    pounded thin, each folded in
    half enclosing 1 to 2
    tablespoons of chopped foie
    gras (or chicken liver pâté),
    the edges of the veal then
    pressed together or fastened
    with toothpicks, seasoned,
    and lightly floured
1 *ounce Madeira*
3 *ounces beef stock or broth,*
    preferably unsalted
1 *tablespoon red currant jelly*
2 *teaspoons cornstarch blended*
    with 1 tablespoon Madeira

• Melt margarine in 12-inch pan. Fry cutlets for 2 minutes on each side over medium to high heat, turning just once during cooking. Remove cutlets to a hot platter and keep hot.

• Add wine, stock, and jelly to pan; heat through and blend with juices quickly.

• Add cornstarch and Madeira slurry and stir in briskly to blend and thicken. Serve hot, spooned over the veal.

Gypsy Veal

3 *tablespoons margarine*
1 *pound veal, cut into small*
    ⅛-inch-thick slices,
    seasoned
1 *ounce dry white wine*
3 *ounces beef stock or broth,*
    preferably unsalted, hot
¼ *teaspoon tarragon, ground in*
    a mortar
¼ *cup lean ham strips*
¼ *cup smoked tongue strips*
    (optional)
½ *cup thinly sliced mushrooms*
1 *small black truffle, thinly*
    sliced (optional)
2 *teaspoons cornstarch blended*
    with 1 tablespoon dry white
    wine

• Melt margarine in 12-inch pan. Fry veal for 1 minute over medium to high heat, stirring briskly and turning pieces to cook evenly.

• Add wine, stock, and tarragon; fry 1 minute more, stirring. Add ham, tongue, mushrooms, and truffle; fry 2 minutes more, stirring.

• Add cornstarch and wine slurry and stir in briskly to blend and thicken. Serve hot.

Veal with Grapes

1 *ounce dry white wine blended with 1 tablespoon apple jelly*
2 *tablespoons margarine*
1 *pound veal, cut into small 1/8-inch-thick slices, seasoned*
1½ *cups halved seeded grapes*
1 *teaspoon cornstarch blended with 1 teaspoon water*

- Combine wine and jelly in small pan. Cook over low heat to melt jelly. Meanwhile, melt margarine in 12-inch pan. Fry veal for 3 minutes over medium to high heat, stirring briskly and turning pieces to cook evenly.

- Add grapes and the wine mixture; fry 30 seconds more, stirring. Add cornstarch and water slurry and cook to thicken, stirring. Serve hot.

Veal Provençale

3 *tablespoons Italian olive oil*
2 *garlic cloves, minced*
¼ *teaspoon parsley*
⅛ *teaspoon rosemary*
⅛ *teaspoon thyme*
⅛ *teaspoon ground bay leaf*
1 *small onion, thinly sliced*
1 *pound veal, cut into small 1/8-inch-thick slices, seasoned*
1½ *cups chopped tomato, salted*
½ *cup sliced pitted black olives*
¼ *cup dry white wine, hot*
¼ *cup chicken stock or broth, preferably unsalted, hot*
1 *tablespoon cornstarch blended with 1 tablespoon cold stock*

- Heat oil in 12-inch pan. Fry garlic and spices over medium to high heat for a few seconds, stirring.

- Add onion and fry 30 seconds more, stirring briskly. Add veal and fry 1 minute, stirring and turning pieces to cook evenly.

- Add tomatoes and olives; fry 2 minutes, stirring. Add wine and stock; fry 1 minute more, stirring. Add cornstarch and stock slurry; stir in briskly to blend and thicken. Serve hot.

Lemon Veal

2 *tablespoons margarine*
1 *pound veal, cut into small*
  1/8-inch-thick slices,
  seasoned
2 *ounces Grand Marnier liqueur*
1 *tablespoon lemon juice*

- Melt margarine in 10-inch pan. Fry veal for 3 minutes over medium to high heat, stirring briskly and turning pieces to cook evenly.

- Flame with Grand Marnier, stirring until fire dies.

- Add lemon juice and fry 30 seconds more, stirring. Serve hot.

Veal and Mushrooms with Mustard Sauce

3 *tablespoons margarine*
1 *garlic clove, minced*
½ *teaspoon parsley*
¼ *teaspoon oregano*
⅛ *teaspoon ground bay leaf*
1 *onion, thinly sliced*
1 *pound veal, cut into small*
  1/8-inch-thick slices,
  seasoned
1½ *cups thinly sliced mushrooms*
2 *teaspoons prepared mustard*
  (or to taste)
1 *ounce dry white wine*
¼ *cup beef stock or broth,*
  preferably unsalted, hot
2 *teaspoons cornstarch*
  blended with 2
  tablespoons cream
  lemon juice to taste

- Melt margarine in 12-inch pan. Fry garlic and herbs over medium to high heat for a few seconds, stirring.

- Add onion and fry 30 seconds more, stirring briskly. Add veal and mushrooms; fry 3 minutes more, stirring and turning pieces to cook evenly. Add mustard and blend in quickly. Add wine and stock and fry 1 minute more, stirring.

- Add cornstarch and cream slurry; stir in briskly to blend and thicken. Add lemon juice (just a few drops) and blend in quickly. Serve hot.

Veal with Peppers

2 tablespoons margarine
1 tablespoon Italian olive oil
2 garlic cloves, minced
½ teaspoon basil
¼ teaspoon oregano
1 pound veal, cut into small
  ⅛-inch-thick slices,
  seasoned
½ cup minced green pepper
1 cup chopped tomato, salted
¼ cup grated Swiss or Gruyère
  cheese
¼ cup bread crumbs

• Heat margarine and oil in 12-inch pan. Fry garlic and herbs over medium to high heat for a few seconds, stirring.

• Add veal and pepper and fry 2 minutes more, stirring briskly and turning pieces to cook evenly.

• Add tomato and fry 2 minutes, stirring. Add cheese and bread crumbs and fry 30 seconds more, tossing mixture until cheese begins to melt. Serve hot.

Warm Spiced Veal

3 tablespoons margarine
½ teaspoon ginger
¼ teaspoon cinnamon
⅛ teaspoon nutmeg
⅛ teaspoon turmeric
1/16 teaspoon ground cloves
1 garlic clove, minced
1 small onion, minced
1 pound veal, cut into small
  ⅛-inch-thick slices,
  seasoned
2 scallions, cut into thin strips

• Melt margarine in 12-inch pan. Fry spices, garlic, and onion for 30 seconds over medium to high heat, stirring.

• Add veal and fry 2 minutes more, stirring briskly and turning pieces to cook evenly.

• Add scallions and fry 1 minute more, stirring. Serve hot.

Speedy Schnitzel

2 tablespoons margarine,
   divided
2 tablespoons Italian olive oil,
   divided
¾ pound thin, pounded veal
   cutlets, seasoned, floured
   lightly, and dipped in
   seasoned beaten egg
2 tablespoons minced capers
   lemon wedges

- Heat half the margarine and oil in a 12-inch pan. Fry half the schnitzel over medium to high heat for about 1 minute on each side. Remove to a hot platter and keep hot.

- Fry remaining schnitzel in remaining margarine and oil in the same pan. Remove to hot platter and keep hot.

- Add capers to pan and stir in to mix quickly with juices. Sprinkle over schnitzel and serve hot, garnished with lemon wedges.

Veal with Tuna

3 tablespoons margarine
¼ cup minced onion
¼ cup finely minced celery
1 pound veal, cut into small
   ⅛-inch-thick slices,
   seasoned
½ can white-meat tuna,
   drained and flaked
3 anchovy fillets, chopped
¼ cup dry white wine, hot
¼ cup chicken stock or broth,
   preferably unsalted, hot
2 teaspoons cornstarch blended
   with 1 tablespoon cold stock
1 tablespoon capers

- Melt margarine in 12-inch pan. Fry onion and celery for 30 seconds over medium to high heat, stirring briskly.

- Add veal and fry 3 minutes more, stirring and turning pieces to cook evenly. Add tuna, anchovies, wine, and stock; fry 30 seconds more, stirring gently.

- Add cornstarch and stock slurry; stir in quickly but gently to blend and thicken. Serve hot, sprinkled with capers.

CHICKEN

Apple Onion Chicken

3 *tablespoons margarine*
¼ *teaspoon cinnamon*
⅛ *teaspoon coriander*
⅛ *teaspoon turmeric*
⅛ *teaspoon fenugreek*
¹⁄₁₆ *teaspoon ground cloves*
1 *onion, thinly sliced*
1 *pound boned chicken breasts,*
   cut into small ⅛-inch-thick
   slices, seasoned
2 *small apples, peeled, cored,*
   and thinly sliced

- Melt margarine in 12-inch pan. Fry spices over medium to high heat for a few seconds, stirring.

- Add onion and fry 20 seconds more, stirring briskly.

- Add chicken and fry 3 minutes, stirring and turning pieces to cook evenly. Add apples and fry 1 ½ minutes, stirring gently. Serve hot.

Quick Chicken Cacciatore

2 *tablespoons Italian olive oil*
½ *teaspoon parsley*
⅛ *teaspoon rosemary*
⅛ *teaspoon thyme*
⅛ *teaspoon ground bay leaf*
1 *green pepper, cut into very*
   fine strips
1 *garlic clove, minced*
1 *pound boned chicken breasts,*
   cut into small ⅛-inch-thick
   slices, seasoned
3 *scallions, cut into small strips*
2 *tomatoes, chopped and salted*
1 *pimiento, cut into strips*

- Heat oil in 12-inch pan. Fry herbs over medium to high heat for a few seconds, stirring. Add pepper and garlic and fry 30 seconds more, stirring briskly.

- Add chicken and fry 2 minutes, stirring and turning pieces to cook evenly.

- Add scallions, tomatoes, and pimiento; fry 2 minutes, stirring gently. Serve hot.

Caraway Chicken with Ham

2 *tablespoons margarine*
1 *garlic clove, minced*
¼ *cup minced onion*
½ *teaspoon caraway seed,*
    crushed in a mortar
¼ *teaspoon basil*
1 *pound boned chicken breasts,*
    cut into small ⅛-inch-thick
    slices, seasoned
½ *cup lean ham slices*
½ *cup beef stock or broth,*
    preferably unsalted, hot
1 *tablespoon red currant jelly*
2 *teaspoons cornstarch blended*
    with 1 tablespoon dry red
    wine

• Melt margarine in 10-inch pan. Fry garlic, onion, and spices over medium to high heat for a few seconds, stirring.

• Add chicken and fry 2 minutes more, stirring briskly and turning pieces to cook evenly.

• Add ham and fry 1 minute, stirring. Add stock and fry 30 seconds, covered.

• Add jelly and blend in quickly. Add cornstarch and wine slurry and stir in briskly to blend and thicken. Serve hot.

Castilian Chicken

2 *tablespoons Italian olive oil*
½ *teaspoon parsley*
⅛ *teaspoon ground bay leaf*
⅛ *teaspoon turmeric*
1/16 *teaspoon ground cloves*
1 *pound boned chicken breasts,*
    cut into small ⅛-inch-thick
    slices, seasoned
3 *scallions, cut into small strips*
2 *tomatoes, chopped and salted*

• Heat oil in 12-inch pan. Fry spices over medium to high heat for a few seconds, stirring.

• Add chicken and fry 2 minutes more, stirring briskly and turning pieces to cook evenly.

• Add scallions and fry 1 minute, stirring. Add tomatoes and fry 2 minutes, stirring. Serve hot.

Cheesy Chicken

2 tablespoons peanut oil
1 garlic clove, minced
½ teaspoon parsley
¼ teaspoon oregano
⅛ teaspoon thyme
1/16 teaspoon ground nutmeg
1 pound boned chicken breasts, cut into small ⅛-inch-thick slices, seasoned
3 scallions, cut into small strips
¼ cup chopped Swiss and blue cheeses, mixed

• Heat oil in 10-inch pan. Fry garlic and spices over medium to high heat for a few seconds, stirring.

• Add chicken and fry 1 minute more, stirring briskly and turning pieces to cook evenly.

• Add scallions and fry 2 minutes, stirring. Add cheeses and fry 45 seconds, tossing very gently to melt. Serve hot.

Cherry Orange Chicken

2 tablespoons margarine
¼ teaspoon cinnamon
⅛ teaspoon nutmeg
1/16 teaspoon ground cloves
1 pound boned chicken breasts, cut into small ⅛-inch-thick slices, seasoned
½ cup halved pitted cherries
½ cup seeded orange sections, peeled of membranes
½ cup mixed orange and cherry juices, hot (cherry juice may be canned, maraschino, or squeezed fresh)
1 tablespoon orange marmalade
2 teaspoons cornstarch blended with 1 tablespoon dry white wine

• Melt margarine in 12-inch pan. Fry spices over medium to high heat for a few seconds, stirring.

• Add chicken and fry 3 minutes more, stirring briskly and turning pieces to cook evenly.

• Add cherries and orange sections and fry 30 seconds, stirring gently. Add juices and blend in quickly but gently. Add marmalade and blend in quickly but gently.

• Add cornstarch and wine slurry and stir in quickly but gently to thicken. Serve hot.

Chicken Chili

3 tablespoons margarine
1 garlic clove, minced
½ cup minced onion
1 teaspoon chili powder
½ teaspoon cumin
¼ teaspoon oregano
1 pound boned chicken breasts,
    cut into small ⅛-inch-thick
    slices, seasoned
¼ pound chopped chicken livers
1 package frozen French-style
    green beans, thawed
½ cup canned mushroom juice,
    hot
1 tablespoon tomato paste
2 teaspoons cornstarch blended
    with 1 tablespoon Madeira

• Melt margarine in 12-inch pan. Fry garlic, onion, and spices over medium to high heat for a few seconds, stirring.

• Add chicken, livers, and beans; fry 3 minutes more, stirring briskly and turning pieces to cook evenly.

• Add mushroom juice and fry 2 minutes more, covered. Add tomato paste and blend in quickly.

• Add cornstarch and Madeira slurry and stir in briskly to blend and thicken. Serve hot.

Spiced Cider Chicken

2 tablespoons margarine
½ teaspoon ground ginger
¼ teaspoon cinnamon
⅛ teaspoon ground cloves
¼ teaspoon anise seed, crushed
    in a mortar
2 tablespoons minced onion
1 garlic clove, minced
1 pound boned chicken breasts,
    cut into small ⅛-inch-thick
    slices
1 tablespoon soy sauce
    pepper to taste
½ cup cider or apple juice, hot
2 teaspoons cornstarch blended
    with 1 tablespoon cold cider

• Melt margarine in 10-inch pan. Fry spices, onion, and garlic over medium to high heat for a few seconds, stirring.

• Add chicken and fry 2 minutes more, stirring briskly and turning pieces to cook evenly. Add soy sauce and blend quickly. Season with pepper.

• Add cider and fry 1 minute, stirring. Add cornstarch and cider slurry and stir in briskly to blend and thicken. Serve hot.

Chicken Fontina

3 *tablespoons margarine*
1 *pound boned chicken breasts, cut into small ⅛-inch-thick slices, seasoned*
1 *cup thinly sliced mushrooms*
1 *ounce kirsch (cherry brandy)*
½ *cup chopped fontina cheese or processed cheese*

- Melt margarine in 12-inch pan. Fry chicken for 2 minutes over medium to high heat, stirring briskly and turning pieces to cook evenly.
- Add mushrooms and fry 2 minutes more, stirring. Flame with kirsch, stirring until fire dies.
- Add cheese and toss quickly to blend and melt. Serve hot.

Green-Pepper Chicken

2 *tablespoons peanut oil*
1 *pound boned chicken breasts, cut into small ⅛-inch-thick slices, seasoned*
½ *cup thinly sliced mushrooms*
½ *teaspoon parsley*
1 *garlic clove, minced*
¼ *cup diced green pepper*
1 *small tomato, cut in thin wedges*
1 *ounce dry white wine*
  a few drops lemon juice

- Heat oil in 12-inch pan. Fry chicken and mushrooms for 1 minute over medium to high heat, stirring briskly and turning pieces to cook evenly.
- Add parsley and blend in quickly. Add garlic and green pepper and fry 1 minute more, stirring.
- Add tomato and fry 2 minutes, stirring. Add wine and lemon juice; blend quickly. Serve hot.

Herbed Chicken

2 tablespoons margarine
1 garlic clove, minced
2 teaspoons chopped chives or
   onion greens
½ teaspoon parsley
½ teaspoon basil
¼ teaspoon oregano
⅛ teaspoon ground bay leaf
1 pound boned chicken breasts,
   cut into small ⅛-inch-thick
   slices, seasoned
1 ounce dry white wine
½ cup veal or chicken gravy, hot
   (optional)

- Melt margarine in 10-inch pan. Fry garlic, chives, and herbs over medium to high heat for a few seconds, stirring.

- Add chicken and fry 3 minutes more, stirring briskly and turning pieces to cook evenly.

- Add wine and fry 1 minute, stirring. Add gravy and stir in quickly to blend and heat through. Serve hot.

Chicken Hot Pepper

2 tablespoons margarine
2 garlic cloves, minced
1 pound boned chicken breasts,
   cut into small ⅛-inch-thick
   slices
1 to 2 teaspoons seeded and
   chopped canned chili
   peppers (or to taste)
2 teaspoons soy sauce
½ cup chicken stock or broth,
   preferably unsalted, hot
2 teaspoons cornstarch blended
   with 1 tablespoon cold stock

- Melt margarine in 10-inch pan. Fry garlic over medium to high heat for a few seconds, stirring.

- Add chicken and fry 2 minutes more, stirring briskly and turning pieces to cook evenly.

- Add chili peppers and fry 2 minutes, stirring. Add soy sauce and blend in quickly.

- Add stock and blend in quickly. Add cornstarch and stock slurry and stir in briskly to blend and thicken. Serve hot.

Creamy Chicken and Leeks

2 tablespoons margarine
1 teaspoon parsley
½ teaspoon tarragon
⅛ teaspoon thyme
1 pound boned chicken breasts,
    cut into small ⅛-inch-thick
    slices
6 leek whites, thinly sliced
    salt and pepper to taste
2 ounces dry white wine
1 tablespoon red currant jelly
2 teaspoons cornstarch blended
    with 2 ounces cream

- Melt margarine in 12-inch pan. Fry herbs over medium to high heat for a few seconds, stirring.

- Add chicken and fry 2 minutes more, stirring briskly and turning pieces to cook evenly. Add leeks and fry 2 minutes, stirring. Season with salt and pepper.

- Add wine and blend in quickly. Cover and cook 15 seconds.

- Add red currant jelly and blend in quickly. Add cornstarch and cream slurry and stir in briskly to blend and thicken. Serve hot.

Lemon Chicken

2 tablespoons margarine
2 garlic cloves, minced
1 pound boned chicken breasts,
    cut into small ⅛-inch-thick
    slices, seasoned
½ cup chicken stock or broth,
    preferably unsalted, hot
1 ounce Madeira
2 teaspoons soy sauce
½ teaspoon sugar
1 tablespoon lemon juice,
    preferably fresh
1 tablespoon cornstarch
    blended with 1 tablespoon
    cold stock
1 lemon, quartered lengthwise

- Melt margarine in 10-inch pan. Fry garlic over medium to high heat for a few seconds, stirring.

- Add chicken and fry 2 minutes more, stirring briskly and turning pieces to cook evenly.

- Add stock and fry 1 minute, stirring. Add Madeira, soy sauce, sugar, and lemon juice; blend quickly.

- Add cornstarch and stock slurry and stir in briskly to blend and thicken. Serve hot, garnished with lemon quarters.

Litchi Pineapple Chicken

2 *tablespoons margarine*
¼ *teaspoon ginger*
⅛ *teaspoon cinnamon*
1/16 *teaspoon nutmeg*
    dash of ground cloves
1 *pound boned chicken breasts*
    cut into small ⅛-inch-thick
    slices, lightly peppered
2 *teaspoons soy sauce*
2 *tablespoons Madeira*
½ *cup canned litchis, drained*
    and sliced
¼ *cup canned pineapple,*
    drained and thinly sliced
½ *cup mixed litchi and*
    pineapple juices
2 *teaspoons cornstarch blended*
    with 1 tablespoon Madeira

- Melt margarine in 12-inch pan. Fry spices over medium to high heat for a few seconds, stirring.

- Add chicken and fry 3 minutes more, stirring briskly and turning pieces to cook evenly. Add soy sauce and Madeira and blend in quickly.

- Add litchis and pineapple and fry 1 minute, stirring. Add juice and blend quickly.

- Add cornstarch and Madeira slurry and stir in briskly to blend and thicken. Serve hot.

Chicken and Mushrooms Flambé

3 *tablespoons margarine*
½ *teaspoon parsley*
⅛ *teaspoon thyme*
⅛ *teaspoon ginger*
1/16 *teaspoon nutmeg*
1/16 *teaspoon ground cloves*
1/16 *teaspoon ground bay leaf*
1 *pound boned chicken breasts,*
    cut into small ⅛-inch-thick
    slices, seasoned
1 *cup thinly sliced mushrooms*
½ *cup thinly sliced, pitted ripe*
    olives
1 *ounce brandy*

- Melt margarine in 12-inch pan. Fry spices over medium to high heat for a few seconds, stirring.

- Add chicken and mushrooms and fry 2 minutes more, stirring briskly and turning pieces to cook evenly.

- Add olives and fry 2 minutes, stirring. Flame with brandy, stirring until fire dies. Serve hot.

Chicken with Oysters

3 *tablespoons margarine*
½ *garlic clove, minced*
2 *tablespoons minced onion*
1 *pound boned chicken breasts, cut into small ⅛-inch-thick slices, seasoned*
1 *cup oysters, drained*
2 *ounces dry white wine*
2 *ounces oyster liquor or clam juice*
1½ *tablespoons cornstarch blended with 3 tablespoons cream*
2 *tablespoons grated Parmesan cheese (or to taste)*

• Melt margarine in 12-inch pan. Fry garlic and onion over medium to high heat for a few seconds, stirring.

• Add chicken and oysters; fry 3 minutes more, stirring gently and turning pieces to cook evenly. Add wine and oyster liquor and blend in quickly.

• Add cornstarch and cream slurry and stir in quickly but gently to blend and thicken.

• Sprinkle with cheese and fry a few seconds more, tossing gently. Serve hot.

Paprika Champagne Chicken

2 *tablespoons margarine*
1 *garlic clove, minced*
1 *tablespoon minced onion*
1 *pound boned chicken breasts, cut into small ⅛-inch-thick slices, seasoned*
2 *teaspoons paprika*
½ *cup champagne, hot*
1 *tablespoon cornstarch blended with ¼ cup cream*

• Melt margarine in 10-inch pan. Fry garlic and onion over medium to high heat for a few seconds, stirring.

• Add chicken and fry 3 minutes more, stirring briskly and turning pieces to cook evenly. Add paprika and fry 1 minute, stirring.

• Add champagne and fry 15 seconds, stirring. Add cornstarch and cream slurry and stir in briskly to blend and thicken. Serve hot.

Chicken with Red Wine

3 *tablespoons margarine*
½ *teaspoon parsley*
⅛ *teaspoon thyme*
⅛ *teaspoon ground bay leaf*
¹⁄₁₆ *teaspoon ground cloves*
¹⁄₁₆ *teaspoon nutmeg*
1 *pound boned chicken breasts,*
    cut into small ⅛-inch-thick
    slices, seasoned
1 *scallion, cut into small strips*
¼ *cup very thinly sliced onion*
½ *cup chopped lean ham*
½ *cup thinly sliced mushrooms*
2 *teaspoons flour blended with*
    3 ounces dry red wine

• Melt margarine in 12-inch pan. Fry spices over medium to high heat for a few seconds, stirring.

• Add chicken and scallion and fry 2 minutes more, stirring briskly and turning pieces to cook evenly.

• Add onion, ham, and mushrooms; fry 3 minutes, stirring.

• Add flour and wine slurry and blend in well until thickened. Serve hot.

Sake Chicken

2 *tablespoons margarine*
1 *pound boned chicken breasts,*
    cut into small ⅛-inch-thick
    slices
    salt and pepper to taste
½ *cup sake, hot*
2 *teaspoons cider vinegar*
1 *teaspoon sugar*
2 *teaspoons prepared mustard*
2 *teaspoons cornstarch blended*
    with 1 tablespoon cold sake

• Melt margarine in 10-inch pan. Fry chicken for 2 minutes over medium to high heat, stirring briskly and turning pieces to cook evenly. Season with salt and pepper.

• Add sake and fry 1 minute more, stirring. Add vinegar and blend in quickly. Add sugar and blend in quickly.

• Add mustard and blend in quickly. Add cornstarch and sake slurry and stir in briskly to blend and thicken. Serve hot.

Sesame Chive Chicken

2 *tablespoons peanut oil*
1 *tablespoon sesame seed*
1 *pound boned chicken breasts,
    cut into small ⅛-inch-thick
    slices*
¼ *cup chopped chives or green
    onion tops*
   pepper to taste
1 *tablespoon soy sauce*
2 *ounces Madeira*
2 *teaspoons cornstarch blended
    with 2 ounces milk*

• Heat oil in 10-inch pan. Fry sesame seed over medium to high heat for 15 seconds, stirring.

• Add chicken and fry 2 minutes more, stirring briskly and turning pieces to cook evenly.

• Add chives and fry 30 seconds, stirring. Season with pepper, stirring continuously. Add soy sauce and blend in quickly.

• Add Madeira and blend in quickly; then cover and cook 15 seconds. Add cornstarch and milk slurry and stir in briskly to blend and thicken. Serve hot.

Sherry Chicken

2 *tablespoons margarine*
½ *teaspoon parsley*
¼ *teaspoon basil*
⅛ *teaspoon thyme*
1 *pound boned chicken breasts,
    cut into small ⅛-inch-thick
    slices, seasoned*
¼ *cup beef stock or broth,
    preferably unsalted, hot*
¼ *cup sherry, hot*
2 *teaspoons cornstarch blended
    with 1 tablespoon cold
    sherry*

• Melt margarine in 10-inch pan. Fry herbs over medium to high heat for a few seconds, stirring.

• Add chicken and fry 3 minutes more, stirring briskly and turning pieces to cook evenly. Add the stock and sherry and cook another 30 seconds, stirring.

• Add cornstarch and sherry slurry; stir in briskly to blend and thicken. Serve hot.

Chicken Sour Almond

2 *tablespoons margarine*
½ *teaspoon parsley*
⅛ *teaspoon thyme*
⅛ *teaspoon ground bay leaf*
⅛ *teaspoon nutmeg*
1/16 *teaspoon mace*
1 *garlic clove, minced*
½ *cup slivered almonds*
1 *pound boned chicken breasts,*
   cut into small ⅛-inch-thick
   slices, seasoned
½ *cup sour cream blended with*
   1 ounce Madeira

- Melt margarine in 12-inch pan. Fry spices and garlic over medium to high heat for a few seconds, stirring.

- Add almonds and chicken and fry 3 minutes more, stirring briskly and turning pieces to cook evenly.

- Add sour cream mixture and blend in quickly to heat through. Serve hot.

Warm Spiced Chicken

2 *tablespoons margarine*
½ *teaspoon cinnamon*
¼ *teaspoon nutmeg*
¼ *teaspoon turmeric*
⅛ *teaspoon ground cloves*
1 *garlic clove, minced*
½ *cup minced onion*
1 *pound boned chicken breasts,*
   cut into small ⅛-inch-thick
   slices, seasoned
½ *cup chicken stock or broth,*
   preferably unsalted, hot
2 *teaspoons cornstarch blended*
   with 1 ounce dry white
   wine

- Melt margarine in 10-inch pan. Fry spices, garlic, and onion over medium to high heat for 30 seconds, stirring.

- Add chicken and fry 3 minutes more, stirring briskly and turning pieces to cook evenly.

- Add stock and fry a few seconds, covered. Add cornstarch and wine slurry and stir in briskly to blend and thicken. Serve hot.

Tarragon Chicken

2 *tablespoons margarine*
1 *teaspoon tarragon*
1 *pound boned chicken breasts,*
   cut into small ⅛-inch-thick
   slices, seasoned
1 *ounce brandy*
¼ *cup dry white wine*
½ *cup chicken stock or broth,*
   preferably unsalted, hot
1 *tablespoon cornstarch*
   blended with 1 tablespoon
   dry white wine

• Melt margarine in 10-inch pan. Fry tarragon over medium to high heat for a few seconds, stirring.

• Add chicken and fry 3 minutes more, stirring briskly and turning pieces to cook evenly. Flame with brandy, stirring until fire dies.

• Add wine and blend in quickly. Add stock and fry 1 minute, stirring.

• Add cornstarch and wine slurry and stir in briskly to blend and thicken. Serve hot.

Chicken with Vegetables and Hot Peppers

4 *tablespoons peanut oil*
1½ *cups thinly sliced mushrooms*
½ *cup very thinly sliced*
   bamboo shoots
¼ *cup very thinly sliced water*
   chestnuts
½ *teaspoon ginger*
2 *teaspoons chopped chili*
   peppers
1 *pound boned chicken breasts,*
   cut into small ⅛-inch- thick
   slices, lightly salted
½ *cup sliced pimientos*
1 *tablespoon soy sauce*
   pepper to taste

• Heat half the oil in each of two 10-inch pans over medium to high heat on separate burners.

• Add mushrooms, bamboo shoots, and water chestnuts to one pan and stir quickly.

• Fry ginger in other pan for a few seconds, stirring. Add chili peppers to same pan and toss in quickly. (Continue to stir vegetables.) Add chicken to same pan and fry 3 minutes more, stirring briskly and turning pieces to cook evenly. (Meanwhile, stir vegetables also.) Add pimientos to chicken and toss in quickly.

• Fry both chicken and vegetables 20 seconds more, stirring. Add soy sauce to vegetables and blend in quickly. Stir chicken also. Season vegetables with pepper. Serve with the chicken, hot.

SEAFOOD

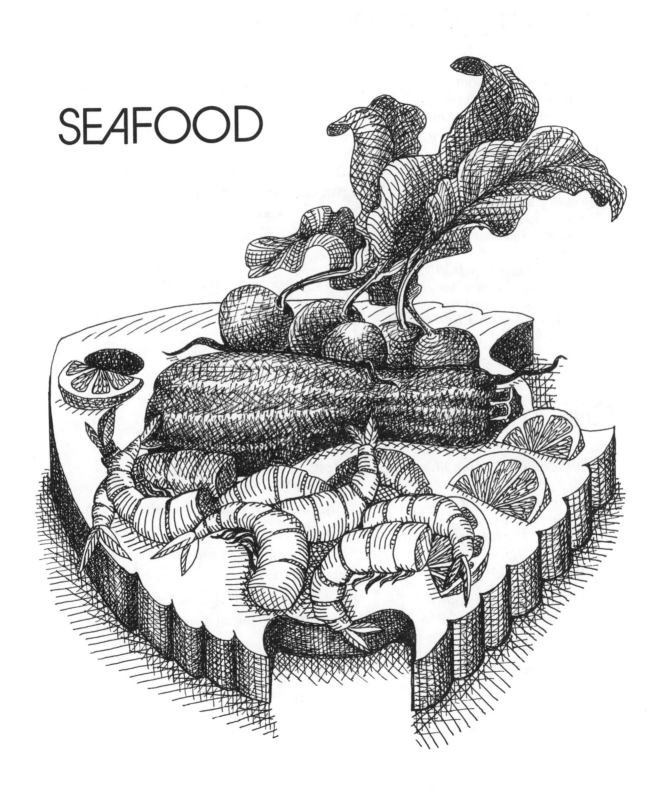

Fish with Bacon and Mushrooms

3 *tablespoons margarine*
1 *garlic clove, minced*
2 *tablespoons minced onion*
2 *lean bacon slices, chopped*
1 *cup thinly sliced mushrooms*
1 *pound thin fish fillets,*
    seasoned
1 *tablespoon cider vinegar*
1 *tablespoon dry white wine*
6 *black peppercorns, crushed in*
    a mortar
½ *cup beef stock or broth,*
    preferably unsalted, hot
1 *tablespoon cornstarch*
    blended with 1 tablespoon
    dry white wine

- Melt margarine in 12-inch pan. Fry garlic, onion, and bacon for 1 minute over medium to high heat, stirring briskly. Add mushrooms and fry 30 seconds more, stirring.

- Add fish and fry 3 minutes, covered, spooning pan mixture over fillets and turning them once during cooking.

- Add vinegar, wine, peppercorns, and stock; fry 30 seconds, stirring, without breaking fillets.

- Add cornstarch and wine slurry and stir in quickly to blend and thicken, without breaking fillets. Serve hot.

Cucumber Fish

3 *tablespoons Italian olive oil*
½ *cup parsley*
¼ *teaspoon dillweed*
1 *cucumber, peeled, halved*
    lengthwise, thinly sliced,
    and salted
1 *pound thin fish fillets,*
    seasoned
2 *ounces dry white wine*
1 *teaspoon lemon juice*
1 *teaspoon prepared*
    horseradish
2 *teaspoons cornstarch blended*
    with 2 tablespoons cream

- Heat oil in 12-inch pan. Fry herbs over medium to high heat for a few seconds, stirring. Add cucumber and fry 1 minute more, stirring briskly.

- Add fish and fry 3 minutes over somewhat lower heat, covered, turning once and spooning cucumbers over top.

- Add wine, lemon juice, and horseradish; fry 30 seconds, stirring in gently.

- Add cornstarch and cream slurry; stir in quickly to blend and thicken, without breaking fish fillets. Serve hot.

Dill Fish

2 *tablespoons margarine*
½ *teaspoon dillweed*
¼ *teaspoon parsley*
⅛ *teaspoon thyme*
  few drops lemon juice
1 *pound thin fish fillets,*
  seasoned
3 *ounces dry white wine, hot*
1 *teaspoon cornstarch blended*
  with 2 tablespoons cream

- Melt margarine in 12-inch pan. Fry herbs over medium to high heat for a few seconds, stirring. Add lemon juice to taste.
- Add fish and fry 1 minute, without turning.
- Turn fish and then add wine. Fry 2 minutes more.
- Add cornstarch and cream slurry and stir in quickly to blend and thicken, without breaking fillets. Serve hot.

Ginger Fish

2 *tablespoons margarine*
1 *tablespoon crystallized ginger,*
  minced
1 *pound thin fish fillets, seasoned*

- Melt margarine in 12-inch pan. Fry ginger over medium to high heat for a few seconds, stirring.
- Add fish and fry 3 minutes more, turning once. Serve hot.

Fish Mediterranean

2 *tablespoons Italian olive oil*
½ *teaspoon basil*
¼ *teaspoon oregano*
1 *garlic clove, minced*
2 *tablespoons minced onion*
1 *teaspoon lemon juice*
1 *pound thin fish fillets,*
  seasoned
½ *cup tomato sauce, hot*
6 *anchovies, chopped*
2 *tablespoons capers*

- Heat oil in 12-inch pan. Fry herbs, garlic, onion, and lemon juice for 30 seconds, stirring briskly.
- Add fish and fry 3 minutes, covered, turning once during cooking. Serve hot, topped with tomato sauce and sprinkled with anchovies and capers.

Melon Fish

3 *tablespoons margarine*
½ *teaspoon parsley*
¼ *teaspoon basil*
¼ *teaspoon anise seed, crushed
   in a mortar*
1½ *cups diced cantaloupe*
1 *pound thin fish fillets,
   seasoned*
1 *teaspoon lemon juice*

- Melt margarine in 12-inch pan. Fry spices over medium to high heat for a few seconds, stirring.

- Add cantaloupe and toss in quickly.

- Add fish and fry 1 minute, covered, spooning cantaloupe and pan juices over top.

- Turn fish and sprinkle with lemon juice. Fry 2 minutes more, covered, with cantaloupe and pan juices spooned over top. Serve hot.

Golden Onion Fish

3 *tablespoons margarine*
¼ *teaspoon ginger*
¼ *teaspoon cumin*
¼ *teaspoon turmeric*
1 *medium onion, thinly sliced*
1 *pound thin fish fillets,
   seasoned*

- Melt margarine in 12-inch pan. Fry spices over medium to high heat for a few seconds, stirring. Add onion and fry 1 minute more, stirring briskly.

- Add the fish and fry 3 minutes, covered, spooning onions over the fish and turning the pieces once. Serve hot.

Fish with Onion-Radish Sauce

3 *tablespoons margarine*
1 *small onion, thinly sliced*
6 to 8 *red radishes thinly sliced*
1 *pound thin fish fillets,
   peppered*
1 *tablespoon soy sauce*
1 *ounce Madeira*

- Melt margarine in 12-inch pan. Fry onion and radishes for 1 minute over medium to high heat, stirring gently.

- Add fish and fry 2 minutes more, covered, spooning onion and radishes over top.

- Turn fish and top with onion and radishes. Add soy sauce and Madeira and fry 1 minute, covered. Serve hot.

Fish with Orange Sauce

2 *tablespoons margarine*
¼ *teaspoon cinnamon*
⅛ *teaspoon nutmeg*
¹⁄₁₆ *teaspoon ground cloves*
1 *pound thin fish fillets,*
    seasoned
1 *ounce curaçao (orange*
    liqueur)
2 *tablespoons orange juice*
2 *teaspoons lemon juice*
1 *teaspoon cornstarch blended*
    with 2 tablespoons dry
    white wine

- Melt margarine in 12-inch pan. Fry spices over medium to high heat for a few seconds, stirring.

- Add fish and fry 1 minute more, without turning. Flame with curaçao.

- Add orange and lemon juices. Turn fish and fry 2 minutes more.

- Add cornstarch and wine slurry; blend with pan juices to thicken, without breaking fish fillets. Serve hot.

Fish Provençale

3 *tablespoons Italian olive oil*
2 *garlic cloves, minced*
¼ *teaspoon thyme*
⅛ *teaspoon rosemary*
¼ *teaspoon fennel seed, crushed*
    in a mortar
⅛ *teaspoon ground bay leaf*
1 *medium onion, minced*
1 *tomato, minced*
¼ *cup pitted black olives, sliced*
1 *pound thin fish fillets,*
    seasoned
½ *cup hot fish fumet or ¹⁄₄ cup*
    each dry white wine and
    clam juice, hot
2 *teaspoons cornstarch blended*
    with 2 tablespoons cream

- Heat oil in 12-inch pan. Fry garlic, herbs, and onion for 30 seconds over medium to high heat, stirring. Add tomato and olives and fry 1 minute more, stirring.

- Add fish and fry 3 minutes, covered, spooning sauce over fillets and turning them once during cooking.

- Add fish fumet and blend in quickly, without breaking fillets. Add cornstarch and cream slurry and stir in quickly to blend and thicken, without breaking fillets. Serve hot.

Schnitzel Fish

4 *tablespoons margarine*
½ *teaspoon parsley*
¼ *teaspoon basil*
⅛ *teaspoon oregano*
¾ *pound thin fish fillets,*
    seasoned and lightly floured
2 *beaten eggs*
1 *tablespoon chopped capers*
2 *gherkins, thinly sliced*

• Melt margarine in 12-inch pan. Fry herbs over medium to high heat for a few seconds, stirring.

• Dip fish in egg and fry 3 minutes in hot spicy margarine, turning once. Serve hot, garnished with capers and gherkins.

Fish with Shrimp Sauce

3 *tablespoons margarine*
½ *teaspoon parsley*
¼ *teaspoon oregano*
⅛ *teaspoon thyme*
⅛ *teaspoon ground bay leaf*
1 *small onion, thinly sliced*
½ *cup slivered lean pork*
1 *pound thin fish fillets,*
    seasoned
½ *cup tiny shrimp*

• Melt margarine in 12-inch pan. Fry herbs over medium to high heat for a few seconds, stirring.

• Add onion and pork; fry 2 minutes more, stirring briskly.

• Add fish and shrimp and fry 3 minutes, covered, turning fillets once during cooking. Serve hot.

Soy Fish

2 *tablespoons peanut oil*
4 *teaspoons soy sauce*
1 *pound thin fish fillets,*
    peppered
2 *tablespoons Madeira*
¼ *cup tomato sauce*

• Heat oil and soy sauce in 12-inch pan. Fry fish for 3 minutes over medium to high heat, covered, turning after 10 seconds and again halfway through cooking.

• Add Madeira and tomato sauce; stir into pan juices without breaking up fish fillets. Serve hot.

Fish with Tarragon

1 *tablespoon margarine*
½ *teaspoon tarragon*
¼ *teaspoon oregano*
1 *small onion, thinly sliced*
1 *pound thin fish fillets,*
   seasoned
½ *cup beef stock or broth,*
   preferably unsalted, hot
2 *teaspoons cornstarch blended*
   with 2 teaspoons cold stock

- Melt margarine in 12-inch pan. Fry herbs over medium to high heat for a few seconds, stirring. Add onion and fry 30 seconds, stirring briskly.

- Add fish and stock and fry 3 minutes, covered, spooning stock over fillets and turning them once during cooking.

- Add cornstarch and stock slurry and stir in quickly to blend and thicken, without breaking fillets. Serve hot.

Tomato-Sauced Fish

2 *tablespoons margarine*
1 *tablespoon chopped fresh*
   parsley (optional)
1 *tablespoon chopped fresh*
   chives (optional)
1 *garlic clove, minced*
4 *tablespoons minced onion*
1 *pound thin fish fillets,*
   sprinkled with a little
   lemon juice, seasoned
½ *cup tomato sauce, hot*
   grated Parmesan cheese
   (optional)

- Melt margarine in 12-inch pan. Fry parsley, chives, garlic, and onion over medium to high heat for a few seconds, stirring.

- Add fish and sauce; fry 3 minutes more, covered, spooning sauce over fillets and turning them once during cooking. Serve hot, sprinkled with cheese, or serve cheese separately.

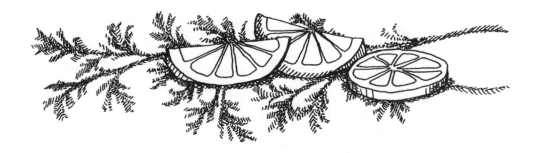

Vinegar Soy Fish

2 *tablespoons margarine*
1 *tablespoon soy sauce*
1 *teaspoon sugar*
1 *tablespoon cider vinegar*
1 *pound thin fish fillets,*
   peppered

- Melt margarine in 12-inch pan. Add, soy sauce, sugar, and vinegar; cook over medium to high heat.

- Add fish and fry 3 minutes, covered, turning after 15 seconds and again when half-done. Serve hot.

Fish and Zucchini with Tomato Sauce

3 *tablespoons Italian olive oil*
1 *garlic clove, minced*
½ *teaspoon parsley*
¼ *teaspoon oregano*
½ *small onion, minced*
1 *cup thinly sliced zucchini*
1 *pound thin fish fillets,*
   seasoned
½ *cup tomato sauce, hot*
1 *tablespoon chopped chives*

- Heat oil in 12-inch pan. Fry garlic and herbs over medium to high heat for a few seconds, stirring.

- Add onion and zucchini and fry 1 minute, stirring briskly.

- Add fish and fry 3 minutes, covered, spooning zucchini over fish and turning fillets once during cooking.

- Add tomato sauce and stir in gently. Serve hot, sprinkled with chives.

Crab with Tarragon Sauce

2 *tablespoons margarine*
1 *garlic clove, minced*
2 *tablespoons minced onion*
1 *teaspoon tarragon*
1 *pound crab meat, cut into*
   chunks and seasoned
1 *ounce dry white wine*
¼ *cup milk, hot*
2 *teaspoons cornstarch blended*
   with 1 tablespoon cream

- Melt margarine in 10-inch pan. Fry garlic, onion, and tarragon over medium to high heat for a few seconds, stirring briskly.

- Add crab and fry 2 minutes more, tossing gently. Add wine and blend in quickly but gently. Add milk and cook 30 seconds, stirring gently.

- Add cornstarch and cream slurry and stir in quickly but gently to thicken. Serve hot.

Almond Crab

5 *tablespoons margarine,*
   divided
6 *small soft-shelled crabs,*
   cleaned, seasoned, and
   lightly floured
¼ *cup slivered almonds*
1 *tablespoon cider vinegar*
1 *teaspoon lemon juice*
2 *tablespoons cream*

• Melt 4 tablespoons of the margarine in a 12-inch pan. Fry crabs for 5 minutes over low to medium heat, turning once during cooking.

• Meanwhile, melt remaining tablespoon margarine in a 10-inch pan. Fry almonds about 2 minutes over medium to high heat until lightly browned.

• Add vinegar and lemon juice to almonds and boil about 1 minute, until liquid evaporates.

• Add cream to almonds and boil about 2 minutes until liquid is reduced by half. Serve crabs hot, topped with almond sauce.

Flamed Crab Meat

2 *tablespoons margarine*
1 *pound crab meat, cut into*
   chunks and seasoned
1 *ounce brandy*
½ *cup fish stock or ¼ cup each*
   dry white wine and clam
   juice, hot
2 *teaspoons cornstarch blended*
   with 1 tablespoon water
   lemon wedges

• Melt margarine in 10-inch pan. Fry crab meat for 2 minutes over medium to high heat, tossing gently to cook evenly. Flame with brandy, stirring gently until fire dies.

• Add fish stock and fry 1 minute, tossing gently.

• Add cornstarch and water slurry and stir in quickly but gently to blend and thicken. Serve hot, garnished with lemon wedges.

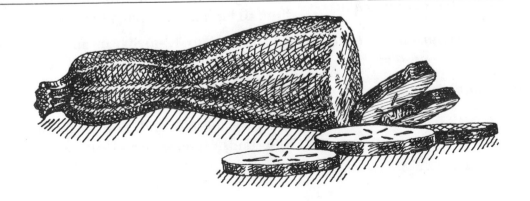

Lobster with Cheese Sauce

4 tablespoons margarine,
    divided
½ teaspoon parsley
¼ teaspoon tarragon
1 pound baby lobster tails or
    lobster pieces, shelled and
    cleaned
    salt and pepper to taste
2 tablespoons flour
½ cup milk, hot
⅓ cup grated or shaved Gruyère
    or Swiss cheese (or to taste)
1 tablespoon cream
    lemon wedges

- Preheat broiler. Melt 2 tablespoons of the margarine in a 12-inch pan. Fry herbs for a few seconds over medium to high heat, stirring.

- Add lobster, salt, and pepper; fry 3 minutes, stirring gently and turning pieces to cook evenly. Set lobster in a hot baking dish.

- Meanwhile, melt remaining 2 tablespoons margarine in a 10-inch pan. Blend flour into margarine over medium to high heat, stirring. Add milk and blend quickly. Add half the cheese and cook until it starts to melt, stirring. Add cream, salt, and pepper and blend quickly.

- Spoon the sauce over the lobster. Sprinkle with remaining cheese and glaze under the broiler about 1 minute. Serve at once, garnished with lemon wedges.

Lobster with Coconut

¼ cup shredded coconut
2 tablespoons margarine
½ teaspoon ginger
¼ teaspoon turmeric
⅛ teaspoon coriander
1 garlic clove, minced
1 small onion, minced
1 pound lobster, cut into chunks
    salt to taste
    red pepper (cayenne) to taste
1 ounce curaçao (orange
    liqueur)
½ cup tomato sauce

- Fry coconut in 10-inch pan over medium heat, until browned, stirring. (Fry dry, using no fat. Once coconut starts to brown, it can burn easily; fry only a couple minutes.) Set aside.

- Meanwhile, melt margarine in a 12-inch pan. Fry spices, garlic, and onion for 30 seconds over medium to high heat, stirring briskly.

- Add lobster to 12-inch pan and fry 2 minutes, stirring and turning pieces gently to cook evenly. Season with salt and red pepper. Flame lobster with Curaçao, stirring gently until fire dies.

- Add tomato sauce and coconut to lobster and fry 30 seconds more, stirring gently. Serve hot.

Quick Lobster Tail Cantonese

3 *tablespoons margarine*
1 *garlic clove, minced*
1 *cup lean pork strips, thinly sliced*
1 *tablespoon soy sauce*
1 *pound baby lobster tails, shelled and cleaned*
¾ *cup chicken stock or broth, preferably unsalted, hot pepper to taste*
1 *ounce Madeira*
1 *tablespoon cornstarch blended with 1 tablespoon cold stock*
1 *egg, beaten*

- Melt margarine in 12-inch pan. Fry garlic, pork, and soy sauce for 1 minute over medium to high heat, stirring and turning pork strips to cook evenly.

- Add lobster and fry 2 minutes, stirring and turning tails to cook evenly.

- Add stock, pepper, and Madeira and fry 1 minute, stirring.

- Add cornstarch and stock slurry and stir in briskly to thicken. Stir in egg briskly and serve hot.

Lobster with Tomato Sauce

2 *tablespoons margarine*
1 *garlic clove, minced*
2 *tablespoons minced onion*
½ *teaspoon parsley*
½ *teaspoon basil*
¼ *teaspoon oregano*
¼ *teaspoon ground bay leaf*
1 *pound of lobster chunks, seasoned*
1½ *ounces brandy*
1½ *cups chopped tomato, mashed and seasoned*
½ *cup beef stock or broth, preferably unsalted, hot*
4 *teaspoons cornstarch blended with 1 ounce Madeira*

- Melt margarine in 12-inch pan. Fry garlic, onion, and herbs over medium to high heat for a few seconds, stirring.

- Add lobster and fry 1 minute, stirring gently and turning pieces to cook evenly. Flame with brandy, tossing gently until fire dies.

- Add tomato and fry 2 minutes, stirring gently. Add stock and fry 1 minute, stirring gently.

- Add cornstarch and Madeira slurry and stir in gently but quickly to thicken. Serve hot.

Spicy Lobster

3 *tablespoons margarine*
1 *garlic clove, minced*
2 *tablespoons minced onion*
1 *teaspoon chives*
½ *teaspoon parsley*
⅛ *teaspoon paprika*
⅛ *teaspoon turmeric*
⅛ *teaspoon cumin*
⅟₁₆ *teaspoon cinnamon*
   pinch of red pepper
      (cayenne)
½ *teaspoon salt (or to taste)*
¾ *pound sliced or chunked*
      lobster meat or baby tails,
      shelled and cleaned
   few drops of lemon juice
1 *ounce Pernod*
3 *ounces chicken stock or broth*
      blended with 1 teaspoon
      prepared mustard, hot
2 *teaspoons cornstarch blended*
      with 1 tablespoon cream

- Melt margarine in 10-inch pan. Fry garlic, onion, chives, and spices over medium to high heat for a few seconds, stirring.

- Add lobster and fry 2 minutes, stirring gently and turning pieces to cook evenly.

- Sprinkle with lemon juice. Flame with the Pernod, stirring gently until fire dies. Add stock and fry 1 minute, stirring gently.

- Add cornstarch and cream slurry and stir in quickly but gently to thicken. Serve hot.

Scallops and Mushrooms with Beer

3 *tablespoons margarine*
1 *garlic clove, minced*
2 *tablespoons minced onion*
½ *teaspoon parsley*
¼ *teaspoon basil*
1 *pound scallops, thinly sliced*
      and seasoned
1½ *cups thinly sliced mushrooms*
½ *cup beer, hot*
1 *tablespoon apple jelly*
2 *teaspoons cornstarch*
      blended with 1 tablespoon
      cold beer

- Melt margarine in 12-inch pan. Fry garlic, onion, and herbs over medium to high heat for a few seconds, stirring.

- Add scallops and fry 1 minute, stirring gently and turning pieces to cook evenly.

- Add mushrooms and fry 2 minutes, stirring gently. Add beer and cook 1 minute, stirring. Add apple jelly and blend in quickly but gently.

- Add cornstarch and beer slurry and stir in quickly but gently to blend and thicken. Serve hot.

Scallops with Wine Sauce

2 tablespoons margarine
1 garlic clove, minced
2 tablespoons minced onion
½ teaspoon parsley
¼ teaspoon basil
⅛ teaspoon thyme
1 pound scallops, sliced and
seasoned
1 teaspoon lemon juice
¼ cup dry white wine, hot
¼ cup cream, hot
2 teaspoons cornstarch blended
with 1 tablespoon dry white
wine

• Melt margarine in 12-inch pan. Fry garlic, onion, and herbs over medium to high heat for a few seconds, stirring.

• Add scallops and fry 2 minutes, stirring. Sprinkle with lemon juice.

• Add wine and cream and cook 1 minute, stirring. Add cornstarch and wine slurry and stir in quickly but gently to thicken. Serve hot.

Curried Shrimp

3 tablespoons margarine
¼ teaspoon ginger
¼ teaspoon cumin
¼ teaspoon coriander
⅛ teaspoon turmeric
⅛ teaspoon cinnamon
dash of ground cloves
¼ teaspoon fennel seed, crushed
in a mortar
2 garlic cloves, minced
1 medium onion, minced
1 pound shrimp, shelled and
cleaned, seasoned
1 teaspoon cider vinegar
½ cup beef stock or broth,
preferably unsalted, hot
2 teaspoons cornstarch blended
with 1 tablespoon cold stock

• Melt margarine in 12-inch pan. Fry spices and garlic over medium to high heat for a few seconds, stirring. Add onion and fry 30 seconds, stirring briskly.

• Add shrimp and fry 3 minutes, stirring and turning pieces to cook evenly.

• Add vinegar and blend in quickly. Add stock and fry 30 seconds, stirring. Add cornstarch and stock slurry and stir in quickly to blend and thicken. Serve hot.

Shrimp with Dill Sauce

2 tablespoons margarine
¼ teaspoon ginger
⅛ teaspoon coriander
⅛ teaspoon cumin
⅛ teaspoon mustard seed, crushed in a mortar
1 teaspoon dillweed
1 pound shrimp, shelled and cleaned, seasoned
1 teaspoon lemon juice

• Melt margarine in 10-inch pan. Fry spices over medium to high heat for a few seconds, stirring.

• Add shrimp and fry 2 minutes, stirring and turning pieces to cook evenly.

• Sprinkle with lemon juice and fry 30 seconds, stirring. Serve hot.

Gibraltar Shrimp

3 tablespoons margarine
1 garlic clove, minced
¼ teaspoon minced chili pepper
½ small onion, minced
½ teaspoon parsley
¼ teaspoon oregano
1 pound shrimp, shelled and cleaned, seasoned
2 ounces dry white wine
2 teaspoons cider vinegar
1 tomato, finely chopped
¼ cup pitted black olives, thinly sliced
2 teaspoons cornstarch blended with 1 tablespoon water
3 anchovy fillets, chopped
1 tablespoon chopped capers

• Melt margarine in 12-inch pan. Fry garlic, chili pepper, onion, and spices over medium to high heat for a few seconds, stirring.

• Add shrimp and fry 1 minute, stirring and turning pieces to cook evenly.

• Add wine and vinegar and blend quickly. Add tomato and olives and fry 3 minutes, stirring.

• Add cornstarch and water slurry and stir in quickly to blend and thicken. Serve hot, sprinkled with anchovies and capers.

Shrimp with Snow Peas

3 *tablespoons margarine*
1 *tablespoon crystallized*
   ginger, minced
1 *tablespoon sesame seed,*
   crushed in a mortar
1 *pound shrimp, shelled and*
   cleaned
1 *package (6½ ounces) frozen*
   snow peas, thawed
1½ *tablespoons soy sauce*
3 *tablespoons sake*
   pepper to taste
½ *cup chicken stock or broth,*
   preferably unsalted, hot
1 *tablespoon cornstarch*
   blended with 1 tablespoon
   sake

- Melt margarine in 12-inch pan. Fry ginger and sesame seed over medium to high heat for a few seconds, stirring.

- Add shrimp and snow peas and fry 3 minutes, stirring and turning to cook evenly.

- Add soy sauce, sake, pepper, and stock; fry a few seconds, stirring.

- Add cornstarch and sake slurry and stir in briskly to blend and thicken. Serve hot.

Soy Scallion Shrimp

2 *tablespoons margarine*
½ *teaspoon ginger*
1 *pound shrimp, shelled and*
   cleaned
1 *tablespoon soy sauce*
2 *tablespoons Madeira*
3 *scallions, cut into thin strips*

- Melt margarine in 10-inch pan. Fry ginger over medium to high heat for a few seconds, stirring.

- Add shrimp and fry 1 minute, stirring and turning pieces to cook evenly.

- Add soy sauce and Madeira and fry 30 seconds, stirring. Add scallions and fry 2 minutes, stirring. Serve hot.

Spicy Shrimp

3 *tablespoons margarine*
1 *medium onion, thinly sliced*
1 *garlic clove, minced*
½ *teaspoon oregano*
¼ *teaspoon savory*
1 *pound shrimp, shelled and cleaned*
2 *teaspoons prepared mustard blended with 1 teaspoon lemon juice and 2 tablespoons thick, rich chicken stock or gravy*
Worcestershire sauce to taste

- Melt margarine in 12-inch pan. Fry onion, garlic, and herbs for 30 seconds over medium to high heat, stirring briskly.

- Add shrimp and fry 3 minutes, stirring and turning pieces to cook evenly.

- Add mustard mixture and blend in well. Season with Worcestershire and serve hot.

Whole Spiced Shrimp

3 *tablespoons margarine*
4 *garlic cloves, split lengthwise*
2 *teaspoons coarsely chopped crystallized ginger*
10 *peppercorns*
1 *small cinnamon stick*
3 *whole cloves*
1 *bay leaf*
4 *cardamom pods*
1 *pound shrimp, shelled and cleaned, salted*

- Melt margarine in 10-inch pan. Fry garlic and spices for 20 seconds over medium heat, stirring briskly.

- Add shrimp and fry 3 minutes, stirring and turning pieces to cook evenly. Serve hot, spices and all, and discard whole spices as you dine.

DESSERTS

Soft Almond Custard

1 *cup milk*
2 *eggs*
2 *tablespoons sugar*
2 *tablespoons flour*
¼ *teaspoon almond extract*
   pinch of salt
   slivered blanched almonds

- Purée first 6 ingredients in a blender on high speed until completely smooth.
- Cook purée in 10-inch pan about 4 minutes over medium to high heat, stirring until very thick. (Stir quite briskly toward the end to keep custard smooth.) Remove from heat and continue stirring briskly for a minute to partially cool. Serve hot, sprinkled with slivered blanched almonds.

NOTE: *This custard is excellent topped with raisins plumped in hot white wine or rum.*

Broiled Bananas

2 *small bananas, peeled and halved lengthwise*
1 *tablespoon curaçao liqueur mixed with ½ teaspoon lemon juice*
   brown sugar to taste
2 *teaspoons margarine, melted*
1 to 2 *tablespoons minced or ground blanched almonds*

- Preheat broiler.
- Set bananas, cut side up, on a sheet of aluminum foil. Brush bananas with curaçao mixture and sprinkle with brown sugar.
- Dribble melted margarine over bananas and broil for 3 minutes, until lightly browned (about 6 inches from broiler).
- Sprinkle bananas with almonds and broil 1 minute more, or until toasted. Serve at once, hot, with juices dribbled over top.

Bourbon Figs

¼ cup bourbon whiskey
¼ cup dry white wine
½ cup chopped dried figs, or
     ¼ cup each raisins and
     chopped dates
¼ cup cream

- Combine bourbon and wine in 10-inch pan. Add figs and simmer over medium to high heat, stirring about 3 minutes until figs are plumped. (The pan should be fairly dry at the end.)

- Blend in cream and cook 30 seconds more, stirring. Serve hot.

Cantaloupe with Pineapple Sauce

1 can (8 ounces) crushed
     pineapple in heavy syrup
1 ounce Grand Marnier
¼ cup dry white wine
1 tablespoon cornstarch
     blended with 1 tablespoon
     water
½ cantaloupe, peeled, seeded,
     cut into bite-size pieces, and
     chilled

- Heat pineapple and syrup in a small pan over medium to high heat. Flame with Grand Marnier, stirring until fire dies.

- Add wine and heat, stirring.

- Add cornstarch and water slurry to thicken, stirring. Serve hot, spooned over chilled cantaloupe.

Cherries Romanoff

½ (1-pound) can pitted sweet
     cherries, drained
3 tablespoons curaçao liqueur
3 tablespoons sugar
3 tablespoons orange juice
1 tablespoon cornstarch
     blended with 1 tablespoon
     water
4 ladyfingers, split
¼ cup heavy cream, whipped

- Heat cherries, curaçao, sugar, and orange juice in a pot over medium to high heat, stirring gently but steadily, until sugar melts completely.

- Blend in cornstarch and water slurry to thicken, stirring gently.

- Remove from heat and cool almost to room temperature. (To cool quickly, set pot in a pan of cold water and stir cherry mixture.) Spoon over ladyfingers and top with whipped cream.

Chiffon Dessert Omelet

4 *eggs*
2 *tablespoons liqueur of your choice*
2 *tablespoons sugar*
3 *tablespoons margarine*

• Combine eggs, liqueur, and sugar in a blender.

• Melt margarine in 12-inch pan over medium heat.

• Purée eggs in blender for a few seconds, just until they foam. Pour eggs at once into hot pan, cover immediately, and cook flat or folded until done, about 4 minutes. Serve at once, hot.

NOTE: *This omelet is exquisite when filled and/or topped with fruits and their syrup. If using canned or frozen fruit, heat some of their syrup in a pan with a teaspoon or two of liqueur, thickening the juices with a cornstarch and water slurry. If using fresh fruits, cook them in sugar and a little water. This can easily be done while the omelet cooks, since the fruit needs only to be heated through.*

Fruits with Raspberry-Currant Sauce

½ *(1-pound) can red raspberries in syrup, drained*
2 *tablespoons red currant jelly*
1 *tablespoon sugar*
1½ *cups chilled mixed fruits, fresh or canned, in bite-size pieces (peaches, blackberries, apricots, plums, seedless grapes, pitted cherries, pears, bananas, or any combination)*

• Combine raspberries, jelly, and sugar in a 10-inch pan. Cook mixture over medium to high heat until jelly and sugar are melted, stirring and mashing raspberries with a fork.

• Spoon sauce (hot or chilled, strained if desired) over mixed fruits and serve.

Ladyfingers with Chocolate Coconut Cream

⅓ cup flaked coconut
¼ cup milk or cream
1 tablespoon rum
1 teaspoon cocoa powder
2 teaspoons sugar
1 teaspoon cornstarch blended
    with 1 teaspoon milk
4 ladyfingers, split lengthwise
4 teaspoons liqueur of your
    choice

- Preheat broiler.

- Simmer coconut, milk, rum, cocoa, and sugar for 2 minutes in a small pot over medium to high heat, stirring.

- Add cornstarch and milk slurry and cook to thicken, stirring. Set off heat and keep hot.

- Set ladyfinger halves, cut side up, on a sheet of aluminum foil or on a cookie sheet. Sprinkle with liqueur and top with the chocolate coconut cream. Toast under broiler about a minute, until just lightly browned. Serve hot.

NOTE: *Try using 4 different liqueurs, so each serving has 4 differently flavored ladyfingers. To further garnish, top ladyfingers with maraschino cherry halves.*

Hot Mandarin Orange Cup

½ cup water
1 can (11 ounces) mandarin
    oranges, with syrup
2 tablespoons sugar
1 tablespoon cornstarch
    blended with 1 tablespoon
    water

- Combine water, oranges and their syrup, and sugar in a small pan. Bring to a boil and then simmer 2 minutes over medium to high heat, stirring constantly.

- Add cornstarch and water slurry to thicken. Serve hot, in cups or bowls.

Quick Dessert Pancakes *makes about 8 small pancakes*

2 *tablespoons margarine,*
    divided
¼ *cup milk*
1 *egg*
¼ *cup flour*
    pinch of salt
1 *tablespoon liqueur of your*
    choice
1½ *teaspoons sugar*

- Purée 1 tablespoon of the margarine and the remaining ingredients in a blender on high speed until perfectly smooth.

- Melt remaining tablespoon margarine in 12-inch pan or large griddle. Fry batter in little pancakes over medium to high heat, in two batches. Serve hot with syrup, jam, jelly, or sugar.

NOTE: *For perfectly shaped pancakes, fry individually in one or more small pans (about 4 to 6 inches in diameter).*

APRICOT RAISIN FILLING FOR PANCAKES

1 *can (8 ounces) apricots in*
    heavy syrup, sliced or
    chopped
2 *tablespoons raisins*
1 *tablespoon brandy*
1 *teaspoon cornstarch blended*
    with 1 teaspoon water

- While frying the pancakes, combine apricots and their syrup, raisins, and brandy in a small pan. Cook for 4 minutes over medium to high heat, tossing gently a few times.

- Blend in cornstarch and water slurry to thicken over high heat. Serve hot as a filling and/or topping for rolled or stacked pancakes.

NOTE: *This filling can be prepared while making one recipe of Quick Dessert Pancakes.*

RUM CASHEW FILLING FOR PANCAKES

1 tablespoon margarine
¾ cup chopped cashews,
    preferably unsalted
¼ cup dark rum
2 teaspoons sugar
2 teaspoons cornstarch blended
    with ¼ cup sherry

- While frying the pancakes, melt margarine in small pan. Fry cashews for 2 minutes over medium to high heat, stirring.

- Add rum, sugar, and cornstarch and sherry slurry; cook to thicken, stirring. Serve mixture hot as a filling and/or topping for hot rolled or stacked pancakes.

NOTE: *This filling can be prepared while making one recipe of Quick Dessert Pancakes.*

Chocolate Pancakes *makes about 8 small pancakes*

2 tablespoons margarine,
    divided
¼ cup milk
1 egg
¼ cup flour
    pinch of salt
2 tablespoons sugar
1 tablespoon cocoa powder
¼ teaspoon vanilla extract
½ cup heavy cream, whipped, or
    vanilla ice cream
¼ cup chopped maraschino
    cherries, with juice

- Purée 1 tablespoon of the margarine and next 7 ingredients in a blender on high speed until perfectly smooth.

- Melt remaining tablespoon margarine in 12-inch pan or large griddle in two portions. Fry batter in little pancakes over medium to high heat, in two batches. Serve hot, topped with whipped cream or ice cream and sprinkled with maraschino cherries and juice to taste.

NOTE: *For perfectly shaped pancakes, fry individually in one or more small pans (about 4 to 6 inches in diameter).*

ICE CREAM PANCAKES

Prepare one recipe of any dessert pancake and serve piping hot, in stacks topped with the ice cream of your choice. If you wish, partly soften the ice cream by letting it stand in the refrigerator for a while before serving.

Peaches Jubilee

½ (1-pound) can peaches,
  sliced, half of syrup
  reserved
1 tablespoon cognac or brandy
1 tablespoon curaçao liqueur
1½ teaspoons cornstarch
  blended with 1½ teaspoons
  water
  vanilla ice cream

• Simmer peaches and their syrup with cognac and curaçao for a few minutes in a 10-inch pan over medium to high heat, tossing gently.

• Add cornstarch and water slurry to thicken. Let peaches partially cool off heat and then spoon over vanilla ice cream and serve at once.

Pears Grand Marnier

2 large firm but ripe pears,
  peeled, quartered, cored
1 cup water
½ cup sugar
3 tablespoons Grand Marnier

• Combine pears, water, and sugar in a small pot. Simmer for 5 minutes over low to medium heat, stirring until sugar melts; then cover pan.

• Mix Grand Marnier with 3 tablespoons of the cooking syrup. Pour over pears and serve.

NOTE: This sauce may be thickened with a cornstarch and water slurry before pouring over the pears. Blend 1 teaspoon of cornstarch with 1 teaspoon of water; add to the sauce in a very small pan over fairly high heat to thicken.

Pineapple Blush

1 can (8 ounces) sliced
    pineapple, drained and cut
    into bite-size pieces
¼ cup maraschino cherry juice
1 ounce dry red wine
    (preferably burgundy)
1 ounce kirsch
8 maraschino cherries, halved
½ tablespoon cornstarch
    blended with ½ tablespoon
    maraschino cherry juice
vanilla ice cream

- Simmer the pineapple, maraschino cherry juice, wine, and kirsch for 2 minutes in a pan over medium to low heat, turning pineapple once after one minute.
- Add maraschino cherries and simmer 30 seconds more.
- Blend in cornstarch and juice slurry to thicken over high heat, stirring to mix well. Spoon over vanilla ice cream and serve at once.

Raisins with Pine Nuts

1 cup raisins
1 tablespoon honey
2 ounces water
2 ounces dry white wine
¼ cup pine nuts

- Simmer raisins, honey, water, and wine in a pot over medium to high heat, stirring until raisins are plumped.
- Mix in pine nuts and serve.

NOTE: This dessert is excellent when prepared ahead of time and served chilled.

Tangerines with Yogurt

1 tablespoon margarine
2 tangerines, peeled, separated
    into sections, and seeded
¼ cup chilled plain yogurt,
    lightly whipped with a fork
¼ cup heavy cream, whipped

- Melt margarine in 10-inch pan. Fry tangerine sections for 2 minutes over medium to high heat, stirring. Let cool for a couple of minutes.
- Meanwhile, gently fold yogurt and whipped cream together. When tangerine sections have cooled, top with yogurt mixture and serve.

Marsala Zabaglione

4 *egg yolks*
2 *tablespoons sugar*
½ *cup Marsala wine*
1 *tablespoon cognac or brandy*

- Combine yolks and sugar in the top of double boiler over gently boiling water. Beat 30 seconds, using an electric mixer

- Add Marsala and cognac and continue beating until thickened, about 3 to 4 minutes. (Do not allow mixture to approach a boil while cooking or yolks will curdle.) Serve zabaglione at once in stemmed glasses.

INDEX